AF683941

A Thorogood Special Briefing

COMPANY ARTICLES AND COMPANY CONSTITUTION

Roger Mason

THOROGOOD

Other Titles from Thorogood Publishing

IT Contracts: Effective Negotiating and Drafting
Rachel Burnett

Managing In-house Legal Services
Mark Prebble

Retention of Title
Susan Singleton

Strategy Implementation Through Project Management
Tony Grundy

Legal Protection of Databases
Simon Chalton

Software Contract Agreements
Robert Bond

Implementing E-procurement
Eric Evans and Maureen Reason

Email – Legal Issues
Susan Singleton

Thorogood Publishing Ltd
10-12 Rivington Street
London EC2A 3DU

t: 020 7749 4748
f: 020 7729 6110
e: info@thorogoodpublishing.co.uk
w: www.thorogoodpublishing.co.uk

A CIP catalogue record for this Special Briefing is available from the British Library.

ISBN: 1-854187 52X
978-1854187 529

Printed in Great Britain by Marston Digital

The author

Roger Mason is a Chartered Secretary and a Chartered Certified Accountant, and a highly experienced company director and company secretary. His career has included periods with the Ford Motor Company and ITC Entertainment Ltd, as well as 14 years as Financial Director and Company Secretary of a leading greetings card company.

Roger now presents seminars on company law, the duties of directors, the duties of company secretaries and on financial topics. He has written 16 books.

Contents

8 REVIEW OF MODEL ARTICLES FOR PUBLIC COMPANIES 93

APPENDICES 113

Introduction

Every company has articles and articles are important to every company. Furthermore every company has a constitution that includes the articles. The company constitution was defined in the Companies Act 2006, the first time that company legislation had done this. It is an important subject and one that is often not fully understood. This Report is for directors, company secretaries, investors and others and I hope that it will be of day to day assistance.

If you read all of the Report, which many people will not, you will probably notice that some subjects are covered in more than one place and in some cases in similar words. This is deliberate and it is because they affect more than one area of the Report, and in recognition of the fact that not everyone will read the entire document.

Company Articles and Company Constitution sounds like a tedious subject and it could be, but I have enjoyed writing this Report. I especially enjoyed writing the first chapter for reasons that I think will be apparent. I hope that you enjoy reading it, but if this is too ambitious an aim, I certainly hope that you find it useful. Thank you for your confidence in Thorogood and myself and with my best wishes.

Roger Mason

Important note concerning terms

Throughout this report:

- CA2006 indicates the Companies Act 2006 as amended
- CA1985 indicates the Companies Act 1985 as amended

A Thorogood Special Briefing

Chapter 1
The evolution of Company Articles and the Company Constitution

- Introduction
- Companies prior to 1844
- Company registration and the Joint Stock Companies Acts of 1844 and 1856
- Limited liability
- Evolution from 1856 to 1985
- The Companies Act 2006
- The number and types of companies
- Development of the constitution and articles
- The 1856 and 2006 model articles compared

Chapter 1
The evolution of Company Articles and the Company Constitution

Introduction

This chapter contains an outline review of the development of company law from Tudor times to the present day, with emphasis on articles and the constitution. It should be interesting, not to say entertaining in parts and the easiest read in the whole Report. There is though a point to it all, because it puts the subject in context and should help in its understanding.

Companies prior to 1844

The earliest companies date back to the sixteenth century and were incorporated by charters granted by the Crown. Such incorporations were few and far between, but they included some well-known names such as the Hudson's Bay Company, the East India Company and the South Seas Company. The East India Company was enormous and a remarkable creation with remarkable powers. It had its own army and Charles II gave it the authority to declare war, something that does not fit comfortably with the now accepted principles of corporate governance. The South Seas Company gave its name to the South Seas bubble, and was a fraud and an unmitigated disaster.

An alternative to a Royal Charter was incorporation by an Act of Parliament. Many companies were formed in this way and it must have taken up a lot of parliamentary time (165 canal acts were submitted to parliament in the 45 years from 1758). Later, the rapid development of the railways led to numerous railway companies created in this way – there were 29 in 1836 and 272 Railway Acts in 1846.

Following the South Seas Company debacle, Parliament passed the so-called Bubble Act of 1720. This Act, whilst commendably aiming to protect the public, severely hampered and deterred the formation of joint stock companies.

Despite this Act the number of unincorporated joint stock companies grew, and their number significantly increased after its repeal in 1825. These companies fulfilled a purpose and had shareholders and transferable shares, but were in a largely unregulated and unsatisfactory position. The situation was ripe for reform. Two Acts of Parliament went some way to help but they had severe limitations. They were the Trading Companies Act 1834 and the Chartered Company Act 1837. These Acts gave some of the features of incorporation, including the right to sue and be sued.

Despite these unincorporated companies most Victorian gentlemen carried on their businesses as sole traders or in partnerships. The great literature of the period gives many unintended illustrations of this. In Charles Dickens' *Christmas Carol*, which was published in 1839, Ebenezer Scrooge is visited by the ghost of his late partner Jacob Marley. He is not visited by the ghost of his late director and fellow shareholder.

Company registration and the Joint Stock Companies Acts of 1844 and 1856

Incorporation by Act of Parliament was prohibitively expensive and not feasible in most cases, and unfortunately unincorporated companies were associated with many fraudulent promotions and other scandals. Parliament responded by setting up a committee to study the problems and make recommendations. This committee was chaired by the youthful President of the Board of Trade, William Gladstone. This resulted in the Joint Stock Companies Act 1844 – often referred to as Gladstone's Act.

This enabled companies to be incorporated by a process of registration, and it established Companies House and the office of Registrar of Companies. Britain was the first country in the world to have company registration. The Act, which did not permit limited liability, applied to all joint stock companies with more than 25 members or which permitted the transfer of shares without the consent of all members. Registered companies had to file basic information and this was available to the public.

In 1855 the first Limited Liability Act was passed, and in 1856 the 1844 and 1855 Acts were amended and consolidated into the Joint Stock Companies Act 1856. Existing companies, except for banking and insurance companies, were required to re-register under this Act. The 1856 Act required all registered companies to file an annual return and is often referred to as the first modern Companies Act.

Limited liability

We often take the limited liability of company members for granted, but in the early days of registered companies it was enormously controversial. There were many scandals and of course they are not unknown in modern times. Limited liability means that shareholders are not liable for company debts beyond the uncalled amount of their shares, and in the case of a company limited by guarantee, the members are not liable beyond the amount of their guarantee. The amount of the liability is often very modest and today 85 per cent of companies limited by shares have a share capital of £100 or less. George Bernard Shaw, the acerbic writer, was once asked what the word 'Limited' at the end of a company's name meant. He replied that a group of gentlemen were advertising the fact that they did not intend to pay their debts.

The 1844 Act only permitted the registration of unlimited companies but this was changed by the Limited Liability Act 1855, introduced by Lord Palmerston's government at the height of the Crimean War. Limited liability was hedged with a number of safeguards, including:

- The company had to have auditors approved by the Board of Trade.
- The word 'Limited' or the abbreviation 'Ltd' had to be displayed at the end of the company name.
- The company had to have at least 25 members.
- There were specified minimum amounts for both issued and paid up capital.
- There were tight rules about dividends and loans to directors.

The Limited Liability Act 1855 was consolidated into the Joint Stock Companies Act 1856 and rather surprisingly many of these safeguards were then removed. Most of them have subsequently been reintroduced, some in a different form. Limited liability was a factor in the expansion of trade and the growth of prosperity (by the standards of the time) but sceptics foresaw trouble and the sceptics were proved right. There were a good few frauds and scandals, and 30 per cent of companies formed between 1856 and 1883 became insolvent. The most damaging insolvency was the bank Overend, Gurney which failed in 1866. It had been a long-standing partnership and was floated as a limited liability company when it was experiencing financial difficulties. The collapse of Overend, Gurney led to a general run on the banks and forced the Bank of England to raise interest rates to 10 per cent. The run on Overend, Gurney was the last run on a British bank until the run on Northern Rock in 2007.

There were contemporary doubts about just how far the principle of limited liability was applicable, but many of them were settled by the House of Lords judgment in one of the most famous cases in company law, *Salomon v Salomon and Co Ltd 1897*. Mr Salomon was a leather merchant and by some accounts a less than reputable person. He had transferred his assets into a limited liability company but the House of Lords found no evidence of fraud or deliberate abuse. Mr Salomon owned most of the company's shares and the others were held for his benefit. Mr Salomon won and the principle of limited liability was upheld.

Since the Salomon case there have been many attempts to what is colloquially known as "lift the veil of incorporation". The cases are decided on the basis of the individual facts. However, it can be said that the courts will not allow limited liability to be abused as a fraud or as a way of evading contractual or other legal obligations.

It is interesting to note that out of nearly two and a half million companies registered on the active list at Companies House, only around 5,000 are unlimited. In all the others the members have the privilege of limited liability.

Evolution from 1856 to 1985

The pattern of company law development since 1856 has been for a series of reforming acts followed by consolidating legislation. The first consolidating Act was not long coming. A series of further acts in the late 1850s were consolidated into the Companies Act 1862, which was the first Act to be given the title 'Companies Act'. As well as consolidation there were new provisions, including permitting the registration of companies limited by guarantee.

Not all law affecting companies comes in Companies Acts and the plethora of legislation regularly made company law harder to use and left us demanding consolidating legislation. A major Companies Act places big demands on the Parliamentary timetable and, despite its importance, is not something that voters clamour for. The last four main Companies Acts were in 1929, 1948, 1985 and 2006.

Of course a very considerable body of case law has developed. A rather startling illustration of this is that more than 1,800 cases are listed in the Table of Cases at the front of Boyle and Birds' *Company Law* published by Jordans. Some of the cases are of great importance and well-known, such as *Salomon v Salomon and Co Ltd 1897*. Others are of much more limited application. An example of one of these is *Ernest v Loma Gold Mines 1897*, which established that the company secretary has no authority to insert the date of the meeting in proxy forms unless authorised by the member to do so. The body of case law continues to develop.

There has been a trend towards more public disclosure, and companies have been required to keep certain information in statutory registers which may be inspected by the public. It became a requirement that accounts be put into the public domain. This started with just an annual balance sheet and then a profit and loss account was added. Subsequently consolidated accounts (if applicable) were required and so was more and more information in the directors' report and elsewhere.

An enormously significant development was the concept of a private company introduced by the Companies Act 1908. Prior to then there was only one sort of company – broadly what we would recognise as a public company. Private companies became (by number) the overwhelming majority. In 1907 there were just 70,000 companies registered at Companies House. There are now almost two and a half million, of which 99.7 per cent are private companies. The burden of disclosure was lessened for private companies, and company law in some respects treated private companies differently. An example is the requirement that public companies must have at least £50,000 share capital, of which at least a quarter and all of any share premium must be paid up before it can start trading or borrow money. There are no minimum share capital requirements for private companies, most of which are grossly undercapitalised.

The Companies Act 1948 created 'exempt private companies' which were distinct from other private companies. These did not have to file public accounts and were given certain other privileges. Their status did not last long and the concept of exempt private companies was abolished by the Companies Act 1967. They were then subject to the increased accounting and auditing requirements imposed on all private companies by that Act. The Companies Act 1981 created new categories of private companies, namely 'small' and 'medium' companies. There were reduced accounting and other disclosure requirements for them. These and numerous other changes were in need of consolidation and this was duly done in the Companies Act 1985. Of course the Act itself made significant changes to company law.

The Companies Act 2006

This is the latest main Companies Act and it is huge. It contains 305,397 words and is the longest piece of legislation ever enacted in the United Kingdom. It was a long time gestating. The DTI set up the company Law Review Steering Group in 1998 with instructions to study the whole of company law and make recommendations. Very extensive consultation took place and the Company Law Reform Bill was introduced into Parliament in the autumn of 2005. Incredibly this was an amending Bill, but it was subsequently withdrawn and reintroduced as consolidating legislation. The Companies Act 2006 received Royal Assent in November 2006.

The Act was implemented in stages on different dates, with the final batch of measures coming into force on 1st October 2009. The Act's provisions relating to the company constitution, including the new model articles, were among the provisions taking effect on this final date.

The number and types of companies

Even a casual glance at the figures must reveal the explosive growth in the number of registered companies, entirely accounted for by the growth in the number of private companies. In 1907, just before the option of private companies became available, there were 70,000 companies registered at Companies House. The million milestone was passed as recently as 1995. The number of companies on the active register in the United Kingdom at 30th January 2011 was:

Public companies	8,156	0.3%
Other companies	2,418,858	99.7%
	2,427,014	100.00%

The approximate breakdown of 'Other Companies' was:

Private companies limited by shares	2,343,614	96.3%
Private companies limited by guarantee	78,000	3.2%
Unlimited companies	5,400	0.2%
	2,427,014	99.7%

The number of companies on the total register in the United Kingdom at 30th January 2011 was 2,657,073.

Development of the constitution and articles

The constitution of companies registered under the Joint Stock Companies Act 1844 was expressed in a 'deed of settlement', which was in many ways similar to the constitutional document of an unincorporated joint stock company. This encompassed the function of the articles of association. Shortly afterwards the Company Clauses Consolidation Act 1845 provided standard provisions of the type included in private statutes of incorporation. These were available, if wanted, to be incorporated by reference.

The Joint Stock Companies Act 1856 abandoned the concept of a deed of settlement and substituted the memorandum and articles of association as the twin constitutional documents. The memorandum provided evidence that the subscribers wished to form a company and take a specified number of shares. It also established the name of the company and dealt with certain specified other matters. Companies are still required to have a memorandum, although under CA2006 from 1st October 2009 it is no longer part of the constitution and its functions are greatly curtailed. There is more about this in Chapter 2.

Model articles were provided in a schedule to the Joint Stock Companies Act 1856 and labelled Table B. Subsequently model articles were issued as part of, or by regulations under, the Companies Acts of 1862, 1906, 1908, 1929, 1948, 1985 and 2006. From 1862 to 1985 the model articles for companies limited by shares were called Table A. There were different Tables for other types of company. The tables were amended from time to time before their replacement.

None of the model articles have been compulsory for any company. Companies have been free to exclude them, adopt them in their entirety or adopt them with modifications. For most companies they have been the 'default provision' which is explained in Chapter 4.

The 1856 and 2006 model articles compared

It is fascinating to put the two documents side by side and see how they compare. Some elements are very similar. For example the 1856 Reg. 46 reads as follows:

> *'The business of the company shall be managed by the directors, who may exercise all such powers of the company as are not by this Act or by the articles of association, if any, declared to be exercisable by the company in general meeting, subject nevertheless to any regulations of the articles of association, to the provisions of this Act, and to such regulations, being not inconsistent with the aforesaid regulations or provisions, as may be prescribed by the company in general meeting shall invalidate any prior act of the directors which would have been valid if such regulation had not been made.'*

This single sentence contains 113 words, illustrating that legislative verbosity is not an exclusively modern phenomenon. The same rule is made by the 2006 model articles (number 3 in all of them) as follows:

> *'Subject to the articles, the directors are responsible for the management of the company's business, for which purpose they may exercise all the powers of the company.'*

Some of the 1856 provisions contravene the present law. For example, Reg. 43 includes '*No person shall be a proxy who is not a shareholder*'. CA2006 gives each member the right to appoint a proxy of their choosing. Some are surprising, such as Reg. 38 which states:

> *'Every shareholder shall have one vote for every share up to ten; he shall have an additional vote for every five shares beyond the first ten shares up to one hundred, and an additional vote for every ten shares held by him beyond the first hundred shares.'*

Perhaps the Victorian pioneers could have taught us a few things. Reg. 70 states:

> *'Once at the least in every year the directors shall lay before the company in general meeting a statement of the income and expenditure for the past year, made up to a date not more than 3 months before such meeting.'*

Furthermore an audit was required, though directors did not have to worry about accounting standards. CA2006 gives the directors of a public company six months to lay the accounts and if, which is not compulsory, the accounts of a private company are laid, the directors are now allowed nine months.

This review is concluded by spotlighting something that is inconceivable today and may come as a surprise to many readers. Reg. 11 of the 1856 Table B states:

> *'Any person becoming entitled to a share in consequence of the death, bankruptcy, or insolvency of any shareholder, or in consequence of the marriage of any female shareholder, or in any way other than by transfer, may be registered as a shareholder upon such evidence being produced as may from time to time be required by the company.'*

This is a reminder that in accordance with the law at the time a woman's property vested in her husband on marriage. I recently came across an example of how this could work in practice. At around this time a well known woman novelist visited her London publisher and collected a payment for her royalties. On the return journey she carelessly left the money on the train but it was handed in by a fellow passenger. She subsequently returned to London to collect it from the Lost Property Office, but it was necessary for her husband to go with her and sign for it. This was because he was the legal owner.

A Thorogood Special Briefing

Chapter 2
The Constitution

- Introduction
- Definition of a company's constitution
- Resolutions and agreements that are part of the constitution
- Registration of resolutions and agreements
- Resolutions and agreements to accompany all copies of the articles

Chapter 2
The Constitution

Introduction

Apart perhaps from a very small and simple operation, any group of people pursuing an activity is likely to need a rule book or constitution. If they have formed a club, they will need agreed procedures for such things as choosing the committee and deciding the amount of the annual subscription. Registered companies have always needed a constitution, but CA2006 is the first Companies Act to include a definition.

The constitution includes the articles, though as explained in Chapter 3 it no longer includes the memorandum. Every company must have articles and for most companies they are the main part of the constitution. In fact for many companies they are the only part of the constitution. Nevertheless the definition of the constitution is much wider than just the articles and includes relevant resolutions and agreements. The articles deserve (and get) a separate chapter. This chapter defines the constitution and concentrates on the resolutions and agreements that may be part of it. The last two sections detail how they must be registered at Companies House and made available with the articles.

Definition of a company's constitution

What is a company's constitution? Depending on the knowledge of the person answering and in ascending order of validity, answers are likely to include:

- What's a constitution?
- Don't know
- The memorandum and articles
- The articles
- The definition given by CA2006 Section 17

Many (perhaps most) people would say 'the memorandum and articles', but as explained in Chapter 3 the memorandum is no longer part of the constitution. 'Articles' is therefore better but it is not right. The correct answer is the definition given by CA2006 section 17. This reads:

> *'Unless the context otherwise requires, references in the Companies Acts to a company's constitution include:*
>
> *a) the company's articles, and*
>
> *b) any resolutions and agreements to which Chapter 3 applies (see section 29).'*

The word 'constitution' has been used in previous Companies Acts without a definition being provided, so this is the first time that it has been done. The word 'include' makes section 17 a non-exhaustive definition. The next section of this chapter details the resolutions and agreements listed in section 29 and also other resolutions that are part of the constitution but not mentioned in section 29.

Resolutions and agreements that are part of the constitution

Section 17 as shown in the previous part of this chapter refers to resolutions and agreements to which section 29 applies. Section 29 reads in full as follows:

> *'1) This chapter applies to:*
>
> > *a) any special resolution;*
> >
> > *b) any resolution or agreement agreed to by all the members of a company that, if not so agreed to, would not have been effective for its purpose unless passed as a special resolution;*
> >
> > *c) any resolution or agreement agreed to by all the members of a class of shareholders that, if not so agreed to, would not have been effective for its purpose unless passed by some particular majority or otherwise in some particular manner;*
> >
> > *d) any resolution or agreement that effectively binds all members of a class of shareholders though not agreed to by all those members;*
> >
> > *e) any other resolution or agreement to which this Chapter applies by virtue of any enactment.*

> 2) *References in subsection (1) to a member of a company, or of a class of members of a company, do not include the company itself where it is such a member by virtue only of its holding shares as treasury shares.'*

CA 2006 and the Insolvency Act 1986 require special resolutions for the following business:

	Source
• Alteration of articles of association	s.21(1)
• Change of company name May also be altered by other means provided for by the company's articles (see s.79)	s.77
• Resolution of a Welsh company that its registered office is to be situated in Wales	s.88(2)
• Resolution of a Welsh company that its registered office is to be situated in England and Wales	s.88(3)
• Re-registration of private company as public	s.90(1)
• Re-registration of public company as private	s.97(1)
• Re-registration of unlimited company as limited	s.105(1)
• Disapplication of pre-emption rights by a private company with only one class of shares (May also be disapplied by the articles)	s.569(1)
• Disapplication of pre-emption rights: directors acting under general authorisation (May also be disapplied by the articles)	s.570(1)
• Disapplication of pre-emption rights	s.571(1)
• Disapplication of pre-emption rights: sale of treasury shares (May also be disapplied by the articles)	s.573(2) and (4)
• Reduction of capital in connection with redenomination	s.626(2)
• Variation of class rights: companies having a share capital (Special resolution of the holders of the class of shares concerned)	s.630(4)
• Variation of class rights: companies without a share capital (Special resolution of the members of the class concerned)	s.631(4)
• Reduction of capital with solvency statement	s.641(1) and 642

- Reduction of capital (court procedure) s.641(1) and 645
- Authority for off-market purchase of own shares s.694(2)
- Variation of contract for off-market purchase s.697
- Release of company's rights under contract for off-market purchase s.700
- Payment out of capital for the redemption or purchase of own shares s.713 and 716
- Opting in and opting out resolutions in relation to takeovers s.966(1) and (5)

Insolvency Act 1986

- Resolution to wind up voluntarily s.84(1)
- Authorise liquidator to transfer assets of company to new company in exchange for securities in the new company s.110(3)
- Resolution to be wound up by court s.122(1)
- Members' voluntary winding up, to sanction liquidator's proposals for a compromise with the company's creditors s.165(2)

These are the resolutions strictly within the terms of Sections 17 and 29. The following are the possibilities encompassed by the word "include".

CA2006 prescribes an ordinary resolution of the members for certain business with constitutional significance. These are:

Source

- To allow directors to allot shares in the company or to grant rights to subscribe for or to convert any security into shares in the company s.551
- To redenominate the company's share capital s.622
- To give authority for a market purchase of the company's shares s.701
- A resolution passed in accordance with regulations passed under Part 21 Chapter 2 (Evidencing and transfer of title to securities without written instrument) s.783
- A resolution for provision to send or supply documents by website Schedule 5, Part 4, paragraph 10

There is one directors' resolution of constitutional significance. It is:

	Source
• A resolution to re-register as a private company in order to comply with section 662 (Duty to cancel shares in a public company held by or for the company).	s.664(1)

Finally there is the possibility of a resolution affecting the constitution passed according to a provision of the articles. Article 4 in all three versions of the 2006 model articles states:

> *'(1) The members may, by special resolution, direct the directors to take, or refrain from taking, specified action.*
>
> *(2) No such special resolution invalidates anything which the directors have done before the passing of the resolution.'*

The same right, in slightly different words, is established by Reg. 70 of the 1985 Table A and it is incorporated in nearly all companies' articles. A special resolution is required so it could be argued that it is within the terms of section 29.

The Act refers to resolutions and agreements. It is likely (and good practice) that changes to the constitution will be made by resolutions. Nevertheless the possibility of it being done by agreement should not be overlooked. Case law recognises that if a group of people are absolutely unanimous, it is not in many instances essential that they act in accordance with the letter of the constitution. This is sometimes called the doctrine of unanimous consent. For example if a company has four shareholders, they travel in the same taxi to visit an auditor and ask him to accept appointment as the company's auditor, they would be effectively acting in this way despite the absence of a resolution. Of course in practice the auditor would be very likely to insist on a formal resolution. Such activities have obvious dangers, not least the possibility of later arguments caused by lack of evidence of the decision. They are best avoided and in any case are probably only feasible if the company has a small number of members.

Such an agreement may be incorporated in a shareholder agreement or it may come about in another way. If an agreement affects the constitution, as defined in this chapter, a memorandum of it must be forwarded to Companies House and must accompany the articles.

Registration of resolutions and agreements

CA2006 section 30 requires a copy of every resolution or agreement affecting the constitution to be forwarded to the Registrar. In the case of a resolution or agreement that is not in writing a written memorandum setting out the terms must be forwarded. These resolutions and agreements are listed in the previous section of this chapter.

A copy of the resolution or agreement must be forwarded within 15 days of it being passed or agreed. Failure to comply is an offence by the company and every officer of it who is at fault. The following is an acceptable example of a document to be forwarded to the Registrar.

(Name) Ltd

Company *(number)*

The Companies Act 2006

Company limited by shares

[Special *(or)* ordinary] resolution[s] of *(name)* Ltd

Passed on *(date)*

At a[n] [annual] general meeting of the company's members duly convened and held at *(address)* the following [special *(or)* ordinary] resolution[s] [was *(or)* were] duly passed.

(resolution)

(resolution)

Dated *(date)* ....

(signed) ....

Company Secretary

Resolutions and agreements to accompany all copies of the articles

CA2006 section 36 requires that every copy of the articles must be accompanied by a copy of every resolution or agreement affecting the constitution. This is not necessary if the effect of the resolution or agreement has been incorporated into the articles by amendment and it is not necessary whilst the resolution or agreement is not for the time being in force. If it is not done, an offence is committed by every officer of the company who is in default.

Section 36 only applies to copies of the articles issued after the passing of the resolution, but it might be considered good practice to provide copies for articles that have previously been issued.

A Thorogood Special Briefing

Chapter 3
The new-style memorandum and the old-style memorandum

- Introduction
- The new-style memorandum
- The old-style memorandum
- Companies registered before 1st October 2009
- Changes to the memorandum
- Company name
- Domicile
- Objects clause
- Authorised share capital
- Limited liability
- Public company clause
- Entrenched provisions

Chapter 3
The new-style memorandum and the old-style memorandum

Introduction

Until 1st October 2009 the memorandum and articles of association were the twin constitutional documents, though it was possible that some resolutions and agreements were part of the constitution too. Furthermore, if there was a conflict between the memorandum and the articles, it was the memorandum that prevailed. That has now changed. The provisions of the memorandum are now part of the articles and all that is left is a short document of record that evidences the intention of the subscribers to form a company and (if applicable) to take shares in it. CA2006 section 17 excludes the memorandum from the definition of a company's constitution.

This poses the obvious question of why the memorandum deserves a separate Chapter in this Report. The answer is that it was a separate document until recently and many readers may instinctively feel more comfortable studying it in this way. The matters reviewed in this chapter are still part of the constitution, though no longer in the memorandum.

The new-style memorandum

The new-style memorandum is for companies registered on or after 1st October 2009. It is a very short, simple document stating that the subscribers wish to form a company and be members of it and, if there is to be a share capital, each agrees to take at least one share. CA2006 section 8 reads in full:

> *'(1) A memorandum of association is a memorandum stating that the subscribers:*
>
> *a) wish to form a company under this Act, and*
>
> *b) agree to become members of the company and, in the case of a company that is to have a share capital, to take at least one share each.*

(2) The memorandum must be in the prescribed form and must be authenticated by each subscriber.'

The prescribed forms are laid out in the Companies (Registration) Regulations 2008, SI2008/3104. The prescribed form for a company having a share capital is as follows:

> *Memorandum of association of [insert name of company]*
>
> Each subscriber to this memorandum of association wishes to form a company under the Companies Act 2006 and agrees to become a member of the company and to take at least one share.
>
> | *Name of each subscriber* | *Authentication by each subscriber* |
> |---|---|
>
> Dated

The prescribed form for a company not having a share capital is as follows:

> *Memorandum of association of [insert name of company]*
>
> Each subscriber to this memorandum of association wishes to form a company under the Companies Act 2006 and agrees to become a member of the company.
>
> | *Name of each subscriber* | *Authentication by each subscriber* |
> |---|---|
>
> Dated

The old-style memorandum

The old-style memorandum applied to companies registered before 1st October 2009 and it was very different from the new-style memorandum that superseded it. The old-style memorandum and the articles of association were twin constitutional documents and, if there was a conflict between the two, it was the memorandum that prevailed. The memorandum was required to contain the following clauses:

- The name of the company
- The situation of the registered office
- The company's objects
- A statement that the liability of the members was limited, if that was the case
- If applicable, the authorised share capital
- If applicable, a statement that the company was a public company
- The subscription clause

It was possible to write additional clauses into the memorandum.

All of the above are considered in turn in this chapter.

Companies registered before 1st October 2009

CA2006 section 28 provides that on 1st October 2009 everything in the memorandum of an existing company, apart from the subscription clause, became part of the articles. This includes any provisions for entrenchment. Companies were not required to do anything and could not stop it happening.

Everything formerly in the articles has effect as before unless (and until) this is changed by the members.

Changes to the memorandum

The new-style memorandum is a historical document of record. It is not possible or necessary to ever change it.

Prior to 1st October 2009 it was possible to change most of an old-style memorandum. However, all that is left of such a document is the subscription clause. This is a historical document of record and it is not possible or necessary to ever change it.

Company name

It was a requirement that the name of the company be included as a clause in an old-style memorandum. This is not the case for a new-style memorandum but it must be included in the headings of the memorandum and articles, and in the registration application submitted to the Registrar of Companies (form IN01).

A proposed company name must be unique and not 'the same as' the name of a company already registered. It must also have the correct suffix, for example 'Limited' or 'Ltd' for a private limited company. There are rules about punctuation, foreign language characters, ampersands etc. There are also the following restrictions:

1. *The name must not in the opinion of the Secretary of State constitute a criminal offence.*

   A possible example would be a name that implies that the company is a bank, unless it has been recognised as a bank under the Banking Act 1979.

2. *The name must not in the opinion of the Secretary of State be offensive.*

   This Report is intended for family reading so no examples are given. However, Anglo-Saxon four letter words are likely to be prohibited. This 'censorship' provides scope for dissatisfaction as what is considered acceptable changes over time.

3. *The name must not in the opinion of the Secretary of State give the impression that the company is connected with central or local government or a devolved administration.*

4. *If the name contains a sensitive word or expression, the necessary approval must be obtained.*

The words and expressions are listed in the 'Company, Limited Liability Partnership and Business Names (Sensitive Words and Expressions) Regulations 2009 (SI No 2615). For example the use of the word 'Vet' must have the approval of the Royal College of Veterinary Surgeons.

There are certain other factors to be considered. Companies House provides extensive and helpful information in its guidance booklet GP1. This may be obtained from the Companies House website **www.companieshouse.gov.uk**

Since 1st October 2008 it has been possible to complain to the Company Names Tribunal (often referred to as the Adjudicator). The objection may be based on the assertion that the name is the same as a name in which the applicant has goodwill, or that it is sufficiently similar to such a name that its use in the United Kingdom would be likely to mislead by suggesting a connection between the company and the applicant. The first application dealt with by the Adjudicator concerned a company registered with the name *'Coke Cola Ltd'*. You will probably not be surprised to know that the application was successful.

Domicile

An old-style memorandum was required to state the part of Great Britain in which the registered office was situated. The possibilities were England and Wales, Wales or Scotland. Since 1st October 2009 it has been possible to register a company in Northern Ireland under the authority of CA2006.

The location of the registered office establishes the law that applies to the company. English law applies to a company registered in England and Wales or Wales. Scottish law applies to a company registered in Scotland.

Objects clause

An old-style memorandum was required to include a clause that stated the objects of the company. The directors had a duty to pursue these objects and no others, and if they did pursue other objects they were acting *'ultra vires'*. If the company suffered as a result of directors' ultra vires actions, the directors could be personally liable to the company for the consequences. However, persons contracting in good faith with the company (so long as they were not a director or connected to a director) were not constrained by the fact that the company was not acting within the terms of its objects clause. This was the effect of CA1985 and it is the current effect of CA2006 section 39, but the effect was and is slightly different if the person was or is contracting with a company that was or is a charity. CA2006 section 42 states in part:

> *'(1) Sections 39 and 40 (company's capacity and power of directors to bind company) do not apply to the acts of a company that is a charity except in favour of a person who:*
>
> *a) does not know at the time the act is done that the company is a charity, or*

> b) *gives full consideration in money or money's worth in relation to the act in question and does not know (as the case may be):*
>
> > i) *that the act is not permitted by the company's constitution, or*
> >
> > ii) *that the act is beyond the powers of the directors.'*

It was originally envisaged that most objects clauses would be short and simple, but this was rarely the case in practice. They were often many pages long setting out in exhaustive detail everything that might conceivably be done. For this reason it was very rare for directors to be held to account for ultra vires actions.

The Companies Act 1989 provided that the memorandum could merely state that the object of the company is to carry on business as a general commercial company. If this is included, any activity of a commercial nature is within the scope of the objects clause. This is only useful for commercial companies and not, for example, for most companies limited by guarantee. There is the further consideration that activities not of a commercial nature might not be encompassed. What about a large donation to a political party for example? In practice many commercial companies have the general commercial clause, but with some extra key sentences added to it.

The position changed on 1st October 2009. Companies registered on or after that date were not required to have an objects clause in their articles and the great majority do not do so. In the absence of an objects clause the objects of a company are unrestricted. Directors are required to act in good faith in the way that they consider would be most likely to promote the success of the company for the benefit of the members as a whole. This is one of their general duties as stipulated by CA2006 section 172. However, companies that are registered charities must comply with charity law and charity law effectively requires them to have an objects clause in their articles.

Although companies are not required to state their objects in their articles and most do not, they are free to do so if they wish. If they do, the effect of the objects clause will be the same as under the previous law.

The objects clause of a company already registered on 1st October 2009 became part of its articles on that date. The effect of the objects clause was unchanged, but from that date it became possible for the members to delete it and for the company to continue with unrestricted objects. Once again this is subject to the proviso that companies that are a registered charity must comply with charity law.

CA2006 section 31 states that unless a company's articles specifically restrict its objects its objects are unrestricted. The previous position was that a company could only do things that were permitted by its objects. It is a subtle difference but it has caused some difficulty and some authorities believe that the courts might not accept an old-style objects clause as restricting the objects for the purposes of CA2006 section 31. To avoid this possible problem some companies incorporated before 1st October 2009 and wishing to have restricted objects have deleted the old-style objects clause from their articles and substituted one that restricts what the company can do.

Authorised share capital

An old-style memorandum of a company with a share capital was required to state (unless the company was an unlimited company) the amount of the share capital and how it was divided into shares. That was the authorised share capital, which meant the total value of shares that could be issued. The issued share capital could be less than, or the same as, the authorised share capital, but not more. After registration the members could increase the authorised share capital by means of an ordinary resolution if they wished to do so.

Since October 2009 there has been no requirement for companies to have a figure for authorised share capital in their constitution, and the great majority of companies registered since that date do not do so. It is possible to insert it into the articles if it is wanted.

On 1st October 2009 the authorised share capital of companies registered at that date became part of their articles. It was and is possible for such companies to remove it from the articles by means of an ordinary resolution of the members. Unless and until this is done the restrictive effect of the authorised share capital continues.

Limited liability

An old-style memorandum was required to state that the liability of the members was limited, apart from the memorandum of an unlimited company of course. This was the simple statement 'The liability of the members is limited'.

In the case of a company limited by shares the liability of a member is limited to the nominal value of his shares. In the now relatively rare event of the shares being partly paid, he would in the event of the company's insolvency be required to pay up the balance. It is interesting to remember that most of the privatisation issues of the 1980s involved the issue of partly paid shares. If, say, British Gas PLC had become insolvent before the instalments were due, all the 'Sids' would have been obliged to pay up. It did not happen of course, but it would not have enhanced Mrs Thatcher's prospects of being re-elected.

In the case of a company limited by guarantee the liability of a member is limited to the amount of his guarantee.

In order to establish limited liability of the members it is necessary for it to be asserted in the company's constitution. The limited liability clause of companies already registered on 1st October 2009 became part of the articles on that date.

Public company clause

If the company is a public company, rather than a private company, this must be stated in its memorandum. All the consequences of being a public company follow from this. One consequence among many is that the issued share capital must be at least £50,000, of which at least a quarter must be paid up before it can start trading or borrow money. Neither CA2006 nor CA1985 specify a minimum amount for the share capital of a private company.

Entrenched provisions

Entrenchment means that something more demanding than a special resolution is required to make a change in specified parts of the constitution. It is now possible to entrench some or all of the articles and this is examined in detail in Chapter 4, though it only became possible on 1st October 2009. It was possible to entrench provisions in an old-style memorandum and this was sometimes done, for example, to safeguard the rights of holders of certain classes of shares, particularly preference shares.

CA2009 section 28(2) provides that a provision in a company's memorandum that was entrenched on 1st October 2009 became treated as entrenched in its articles.

A Thorogood Special Briefing

Chapter 4
Articles

- Introduction
- The compulsion to have articles
- The required form of the articles
- The articles as a contract
- The purpose of articles
- The three options concerning articles
- Model articles
- Model articles as the default provision
- The relationship between articles and statutory law
- The relationship between articles and shareholder agreements
- Authorised share capital
- Objects
- The requirement to provide copies of the articles
- Articles and the Interpretation Act
- The latest model articles in context
- Changing the articles and entrenchment of articles

Chapter 4
Articles

Introduction

As explained in Chapter 2 the constitution includes the articles and as explained in this chapter every company must have articles. For almost all companies they are the main part of the constitution and for many they are, in practice, the only part of the constitution.

The compulsion to have articles

It is compulsory that a company has articles and the Registrar will not register a company unless it has. CA2006 section 18 states:

> '(1) *A company must have articles of association prescribing regulations for the company.*
>
> (2) *Unless it is a company to which model articles apply by virtue of section 20 (default application of model articles in case of limited company), it must register articles of association.*'

The required form of the articles

CA2006 section 18 requires that the articles of association must be contained in a single document and must be divided into paragraphs numbered consecutively.

The articles as a contract

CA2006 section 33 makes it clear that a company's constitution (including the articles) is a contract. Its provisions bind the company and its members to the same extent as if they were covenants on the part of the company and of each member to observe those provisions. However, the terms of a normal contract can only be altered with the consent of everyone who is a party to it. This is not the case with a company's constitution.

The purpose of articles

The articles are the rulebook for the internal management of the company's affairs. They are at the core of the company's constitution and in many cases they are the whole of the company's constitution. They are the regulations for governing the company and set rules for such matters as the relationship between the members, the rights attached to different classes of share and the way that the members make decisions. There are of course numerous other possibilities including the ways that directors are appointed and removed, the payment of dividends and the decision-making powers of the directors.

The three options concerning articles

The three options are:

- To adopt the applicable model articles in their entirety and without modification.
- To exclude the applicable model articles and register a stand-alone set of articles.
- To adopt the applicable model articles but with exclusions, additions and modifications to suit individual wishes and circumstances.

Few companies in practice adopt the applicable model articles in their entirety and without modification. Some companies exclude the applicable model articles and register a stand-alone set of articles. All listed companies do this and they normally exclude the default provision. In practice the great majority of companies take the third option.

Model articles

Model articles were provided in a schedule to the Joint Stock Companies Act 1856 and labelled Table B. Subsequently model articles were issued as part of, or by regulations under, the Companies Acts of 1862, 1906, 1908, 1929, 1948, 1985 and 2006. From 1862 to 1985 the model articles were called tables and the model articles for a company limited by shares was Table A. The 1985 model articles are contained in the Companies (Tables A to F) Regulations 1985 (SI1985/805) and are:

- Table A: Regulations for management of a company limited by shares
- Table C: Regulations for management of a company limited by guarantee and not having a share capital
- Table E: Regulations for management of an unlimited company having a share capital

Until 2006 the model articles were called regulations and came in tables. For no good reason that I can see they are just called model articles under the 2006 Act. The model articles from 1st October 2009 are contained in the Companies (Model Articles) Regulations 2009 (SI2008/3229). They are:

- Model articles for private companies limited by shares
- Model articles for private companies limited by guarantee
- Model articles for public companies

There are no model articles for unlimited companies under the 2006 Act. It should also be noted that (unlike before) there are separate model articles for public companies and for private companies limited by shares.

It has been the practice to issue periodic amendments to the model articles, which is important for the default provision described in the next section of this chapter. There were seven amendments to the 1948 model articles and three to the 1985 model articles. The three amendments under the 1985 Act were:

- The Companies Act 1985 (Electronic Communications) Order 2000 which took effect from 22nd December 2000.
- The Companies (Tables A to F) (Amendment) Regulations 2007 (SI2007/2541) which took effect from 1st October 2007.
- The Companies (Tables A to F) (Amendment) (No 2) Regulations 2007 (SI2007/2826) which took effect from 1st October 2007.

The first of these is to facilitate the use of electronic communications for statutory purposes. The last two were necessary because Parts of the Companies Act 2006 took effect on 1st October 2007 – provisions relating to annual general meetings and extraordinary resolutions for example.

Most companies adopt the model articles, very often with modifications. They have the benefit of being tried and tested and there can be a great deal of confidence in their effect.

Model articles as the default provision

For public companies registered before 1st October 2009 and private companies limited by shares registered before 1st October 2009, the Table A in force when they were registered is the default provision. Default provision is not applicable for other companies registered before 1st October 2009.

For three types of company registered on or after 1st October 2009 the applicable model articles are the default provision. These companies are:

- Private companies limited by shares
- Private companies limited by guarantee
- Public companies

There is no default provision for unlimited companies registered on or after 1st October 2009.

Default provision means that each provision in the applicable model articles applies to the company, unless it is excluded, amended or contradicted by its articles. Silence on a point means that the provision in the model articles will apply. It is 'opt out' rather than 'opt in'. For example both the 1985 Table A and the new model articles say (with definitions and in slightly different words) that a quorum for a members' meeting will be two. This means that it will be two unless the articles say differently.

It is important to note that, unless the default provision has been changed, it is the model articles in force when the company was registered that will apply. This is well illustrated with a trivial example:

- Reg. 9 of the 1948 Table A requires a company to replace a defaced, lost or destroyed share certificate. It may require evidence and an indemnity, and it may make a charge not to exceed two shillings and sixpence (12 pence).

- Reg. 7 of the 1985 Table A is very similar but no charge may be made.
- Article 25 of the model articles for private companies limited by shares is similar as to evidence and indemnity, but allows the directors to make a reasonable charge.

It should also be noted that if a company is registered as a private company limited by shares and if it subsequently re-registers as a public company, the model articles for private companies limited by shares will remain its default provision unless steps are taken to alter it.

Section 20 of the Act establishes the default provision and reads as follows:

> '(1) *On the formation of a limited company:*
>
> a) *if articles are not registered, or*
>
> b) *if articles are registered, in so far as they do not exclude or modify the relevant model articles,*
>
> *the relevant model articles (so far as applicable) form part of the company's articles in the same manner and to the same extent as if articles in the form of those articles had been duly registered.*
>
> (2) *The "relevant model articles" means the model articles prescribed for a company of that description as in force at the date on which the company is registered.*'

It is important to be clear that unless the default provision has been changed by the members, it is the model articles in force on the date that the company was registered. It is not necessarily the latest set of model articles. This means for example that the default provision for a private company limited by shares registered in 1947 will be the 1929 Table A.

It is also important to note that if at the date of the company's registration the relevant model articles had been amended, it is the amended model articles that will be the default provision. So the exact date of the company's registration is important. As explained in the previous section of this chapter there were seven amendments to the 1948 model articles and three amendments to the 1985 model articles. The last two of these took effect on 1st October 2007 and are applicable only for companies registered from 1st October 2007 to 30th September 2009.

The relationship between articles and statutory law

If articles contravene statutory law, the particular article or articles will be void and statutory law will prevail. To take an absurdly obvious example, CA2006 section 854 requires the company to deliver an annual return to the registrar. A provision in the articles stating that an annual return was only necessary every seven years would be void and statutory law would prevail. Rather more realistically CA2006 section 307 states that a general meeting of a private company must be called by notice of at least 14 days. A provision in the articles stating that 10 days notice was sufficient would be void. However, a provision stating that 21 days was required would be acceptable.

On the other hand some provisions of CA2006 only apply if they are not overridden by the articles. An example is section 319, which states that:

'(1) *A member may be elected to be the chairman of a general meeting by a resolution of the company passed at the meeting.*

(2) *Subsection (1) is subject to any provision of the company's articles that states who may or may not be chairman.*'

The relationship between articles and shareholder agreements

Shareholder agreements are relatively common. Such an agreement affects the relationship between the shareholders who are party to it and operates alongside the articles. A very considerable number of matters may be included in a shareholder agreement. Two possible examples are an agreement that the parties to it will not oppose a particular minority shareholder's choice of director, and the appointment of a particular person as a professional adviser to the company. These would be unenforceable if contained in the articles. A shareholder agreement cannot override the articles, but it can be binding on shareholders who are party to it. The company itself has a separate legal personality and can be a party to a shareholder agreement. However, it will not be enforceable against the company if it seeks to stop the company complying with its statutory obligations or exercising its statutory rights.

Articles can be changed by a special resolution or by a more rigorous requirement if the articles are entrenched. A shareholder agreement can be changed in accordance with a procedure specified in it, or otherwise by the unanimous agreement of all the parties to it. A possible advantage of a shareholder agreement is that its terms may be kept confidential. Articles, on the other hand, are registered at Companies House and may be inspected by the public.

The shareholders can always change the articles (subject to due procedure etc) even if the change contravenes the terms of a shareholder agreement. However, a shareholder may be liable for breach of contract if he votes for a change in the articles that contravenes the terms of a shareholder agreement.

It is not clear but it can be argued that in some circumstances a shareholder agreement should be registered at Companies House in the same way as the articles. CA2006 sections 29 and 30 (see Chapter 2) require copies or a written memorandum of the terms of agreements that affect the constitution to be forwarded to Companies House. In practice this is virtually never done.

Authorised share capital

It was formerly a requirement (where applicable) for the memorandum to state the amount of the share capital. Authorised share capital is no longer compulsory but it may be included in the articles. The subject is reviewed in detail in Chapter 3.

Objects

It is no longer necessary for companies to have an objects clause in their constitution, though this is subject to the requirement for companies that are charities to comply with charity law. Unless the objects of a company are restricted in its articles, its objects are unrestricted. The subject is reviewed in detail in Chapter 3.

The requirement to provide copies of the articles

CA2006 sections 32 and 36 require the company on request and free of charge to send any member an up-to-date copy of the articles. Any resolutions of the company required to be filed at Companies House must accompany the articles.

A company registered before 1st October 2009 may comply:

(a) by appending to a copy of the other provisions of the articles a copy of the provisions of its memorandum that are now deemed to be provisions of the articles; or

b) by sending together with a copy of the other provisions of the articles a copy of its memorandum indicating the provisions that are now deemed to be provisions of the articles.

There is no obligation to supply the articles to persons who are not members, though the directors may choose to do so. They can of course be easily obtained by anyone from Companies House.

Articles and the Interpretation Act

The Interpretation Act 1978 governs all Acts of Parliament and instruments made under them. This includes the model articles and it has been held that it includes special articles used in conjunction with the model articles. There have been no reported decisions concerning whether or not it includes a set of articles that specifically exclude the model articles, but it is often assumed that it does.

Under the Interpretation Act words in the singular include the plural unless the context indicates differently, and the masculine embraces the feminine, again unless the context indicates otherwise. This last point sometimes causes offence. The model articles take pains to extensively use gender-neutral terms such as 'that director'. They do though use the word 'chairman'. They commendably manage to avoid the increasingly common but grammatically nonsensical use of the word 'they' to denote a single person.

The latest model articles in context

Chapters 7 and 8 examine the 2006 model articles in detail. This section of Chapter 4 looks at them in the round.

Name of the model articles

What's in a name? Not very much and it is not a matter of substance, but the 1st October 2009 marked a change from a practice dating back to 1862 (and arguably earlier still).

In the Joint Stock Companies Act 1856, model articles were Table B, and the former naming convention started with the Companies Act 1862. The new model articles are known as 'model articles' and not as Tables.

Consultation and notice

BIS (as it is now called) consulted very widely and over a long period, and there were several drafts on the way to the final model articles. Many people, including me, gave their views, and many changes were made to the first draft. You may or may not like the model articles, but it would not be reasonable to complain about the consultation.

The model articles are contained in the Companies (Model Articles) Regulations 2008 (SE2008/3229) laid before Parliament on 17th December 2008. This gave 9½ months notice, so it would not be reasonable to complain about the period of notice.

ORDER AND LAYOUT

The order in which subjects are covered is completely different from the order adopted in Table A. The new order is said to be more logical, though you may think that it is hard to see that it much matters.

All the new model articles, after 'INTERPRETATION AND LIMITATION OF LIABILITY', start with 'DIRECTORS' POWERS AND RESPONSIBILITIES'. Table A starts with 'SHARE CAPITAL'.

PLAIN LANGUAGE

An attempt was made to write the articles in plain and readily-understood language. The subject matter and the use to which the model articles will be put makes precision essential and this, to some extent, also makes this difficult. Nevertheless, you may well feel that the attempt has been largely successful. As an example it may be instructive to compare Reg. 6 of Table A on Share Certificates with Article 24 of the Model Articles for Private Companies Limited By Shares. Reg. 6 of Table A reads as follows:

> *'Every member, upon becoming the holder of any shares, shall be entitled without payment to one certificate for all the shares of each class held by him (and, upon transferring a part of his holding of shares of any class, to a certificate for the balance of such holding) or several certificates each for one or more of his shares of any class, to a certificate for the balance of such holding) or several certificates each for one or more of his shares upon payment for every certificate after the first of such reasonable sum as the directors may determine. Every certificate shall be sealed with the seal and shall specify the number, class and distinguishing numbers (if any) of the shares to which it relates and the amount or respective amounts paid up thereon. The company shall not be bound to issue more than one certificate for shares held jointly by several persons and delivery of a certificate to one joint holder shall be a sufficient delivery to all of them.'*

You will probably need to read this several times in order to understand it.

Article 24 reads:

> *'(1) The company must issue each shareholder, free of charge, with one or more certificates in respect of the shares which that shareholder holds.*
>
> *(2) Every certificate must specify:*
>
> *a) in respect of how many shares, of what class, it is issued;*
>
> *b) the nominal value of those shares;*
>
> *c) that the shares are fully paid; and*
>
> *d) any distinguishing numbers assigned to them.*
>
> *(3) No certificate may be issued in respect of shares of more than one class.*
>
> *(4) If more than one person holds a share, only one certificate may be issued in respect of it.*
>
> *(5) Certificates must:*
>
> *a) have affixed to them the company's common seal, or*
>
> *b) be otherwise executed in accordance with the Companies Acts.'*

MODEL ARTICLES SHORTER THAN PREVIOUSLY THE CASE

The model articles are significantly shorter than Table A. The reasons include the following:

1. Certain provisions of Table A were not in the 1985 Companies Act, even though they were generally regarded as common sense and almost universally followed. In some instances, case law decisions probably made them essential. For example Reg. 38 of Table A requires the notice of a general meeting to specify the time and place of the meeting and the general nature of the business to be conducted. This is incorporated in section 311 of CA2006 and not included in the model articles. It is hard to see how a meeting can take place unless the members have this information.

2. Table A in some places repeated what was specified by the Companies Act 1985. For example Reg. 100 requires minutes of members' meetings to be kept, which was a requirement of the 1985 Act. The model articles do this to a lesser extent. They do not however totally avoid stating the requirements of the Act. For example *'that person ceases to be a director by virtue of any provision of the Companies Act 2006 or is prohibited from being a director by law'*. That is so obvious that one must wonder if it needs to be said. The argument for inclusion is that it is helpful to have all the circumstances leading to a director's loss of office listed in one place.

3. Table A was for both public companies and for private companies limited by shares. It therefore contained provisions that were not necessary for very many private companies. The model articles have separate versions for the two types of company, and for this reason the private company version is appreciably shorter.

THE NEEDS OF SMALL PRIVATE COMPANIES

The great majority of companies are small private companies and in many cases they are owner-managed. This means that the directors are the shareholders. Table A was for both public companies and for private companies limited by shares. This has not been repeated and there are separate model articles for private companies. These do not, for example, provide for the possibility of partly paid shares.

The brevity and relative simplicity of the private company model articles have been generally welcomed, but there are dangers that should not be overlooked.

They may not be suitable without modification for large or complicated private companies. Also it should not be overlooked that some companies start by being small and simple, but progress to become large and complicated.

A GENERAL WELCOME

Inevitably some people have some reservations, but the model articles have been generally welcomed.

Changing the articles and entrenchment of articles

Considerations and procedures when changing the articles are examined in Chapters 5 and 6.

The members 'own' the articles and indeed the constitution, so a change to the articles requires a vote of the members rather than of the directors (although this is often done on the recommendation of the directors). CA2006 section 21 states that a company may amend its articles by special resolution. This is, though, subject to the possible entrenchment of the articles. Section 22 reads in full:

'(1) A company's articles may contain provision ("provision for entrenchment") to the effect that specified provisions of the articles may be amended or repealed only if conditions are met, or procedures are complied with, that are more restrictive than those applicable in the case of a special resolution.

(2) Provision for entrenchment may only be made:

- *a) in the company's articles on formation, or*
- *b) by an amendment of the company's articles agreed to by all the members of the company.*

(3) Provision for entrenchment does not prevent amendment of the company's articles:

- *a) by agreement of all the members of the company, or*
- *b) by order of a court or other authority having power to alter the company's articles.*

(4) Nothing in this section affects any power of a court or other authority to alter a company's articles.'

This means that the whole articles or specified parts of the articles may be entrenched, and that consequently a vote or a procedure or both more demanding than a special resolution will be required to amend them. This could be, for example an affirmative vote of 90 per cent of the members, or it could be a requirement for 100 per cent unanimity. It is not possible to change the articles with a vote or procedure less demanding than a special resolution.

It is not possible to entrench the articles so that they are unalterable. A unanimous vote of the members must override entrenchment. It is also not possible to take away the power of the court to change the articles. This power is very rarely used, but it can be done, for example, consequent to a successful claim of unfair prejudice.

Companies House must be notified if and when articles are entrenched, and also if and when entrenchment ceases. There is more about this in Chapter 6.

CA2006 section 22(2) provides that an existing company may only move to entrenchment by means of a unanimous vote of the members. However, at a very late stage it was realised that this could catch provisions sometimes included in the articles in connection with rights attached to classes of shares. Consequently section 22(2) has not been commenced. An amended section 22(2) may be introduced later. This would require primary legislation and is some way off. So for the time being, a special resolution is sufficient to entrench the articles.

An amendment to the articles must be prima facie for the benefit of the company and not amount to a potential fraud on the minority of the members. So, for example, if a group of members holding 80 per cent of the shares use a special resolution to unfairly disadvantage the 20 per cent minority, then the special resolution may be disallowed by the court.

A Thorogood Special Briefing

Chapter 5

Considerations when changing the articles

- Introduction
- Dangers to be avoided

MEMBERS' MEETINGS AND WRITTEN RESOLUTIONS

- Annual general meetings
- Notice period for general meetings
- Short notice of meetings
- Notice period for a special resolution
- Proxies
- Quorum at a members' meeting
- Voting on a show of hands and polls
- Chairman of a general meeting and the chairman's casting vote
- Written resolutions of the members

DIRECTORS

- Directors' meetings
- Alternate directors
- Minimum and maximum number of directors
- Removal and termination of directors
- Retirement of directors by rotation
- Chairman of directors' meetings and the chairman's casting vote
- Directors' duty to avoid conflicts of interest (CA2006 section 175)
- Directors' duty to declare interest in proposed transaction or arrangement (CA2006 section 177)
- Directors' indemnity

SHARE CAPITAL AND SHARES

- Authorised share capital
- Partly paid shares
- Allotment of shares
- Purchase of own shares
- Redeemable shares
- Transfer of shares

OTHER MATTERS

- Provision for the death of all the directors and members
- Age and other discrimination
- Objects
- Electronic and website communication with members
- Failure to notify contact details

Chapter 5
Considerations when changing the articles

Introduction

Should you change your company's articles? Perhaps not – but you should certainly consider the possibility. It is a good idea to review your company's articles from time to time, though not many people do. Now is probably as good a time as any, and possibly better than most.

This may be particularly true if your company was registered before 1st October 2009 and you have not made changes since that date. The new model articles are generally regarded as being up-to-date and suitable for modern conditions. The model articles for private companies are written with small simple companies in mind and will suit the great majority of private companies. They do deregulate and they do follow the government's mantra of 'Think small first'. Parts of Table A, by contrast, are irrelevant for many private companies. You may well want the model articles in whole or in part, or as the default provision, though there are of course many other reasons for making changes.

On the other hand it is a job, and you are probably not short of things to do.

This chapter starts by spotlighting some of the dangers and possible mistakes that can be made. The great majority of the chapter is a review of some of the detailed changes that might be considered. It cannot of course be a comprehensive list to cover all companies and all circumstances, but it should be of considerable help.

Dangers to be avoided

There may be unfortunate consequences if certain potential problems are overlooked. Dangers to be avoided include the following:

COMPROMISING LIMITED LIABILITY

This is mentioned first because a mistake could have catastrophic consequences, in theory at least. Liability of the members is limited by shares or by guarantee if this is stated in the articles. Unless of course it is an unlimited company this statement of limited liability should on no account be omitted. A statement of limited liability (for a limited company) was a compulsory part of the memorandum until 1st October 2009. On that date it was deemed to be part of the articles, and unless it has been removed it will still be there. Limited liability is established by Article 2 in all the sets of model articles.

A mistake could be made if you exclude existing and model articles, and register a bespoke set of articles.

TRYING TO INCREASE A MEMBER'S LIABILITY

CA2006 section 25 does not allow the liability, whether by shares or by guarantee, of any member, to be increased without his written consent. Such written consent can be given before or after the purported change to the articles.

LEAVING OUT SOMETHING ALREADY IN THE ARTICLES THAT IS THERE FOR A GOOD REASON

Your existing articles may be long, very detailed, complicated and old, or at least some of these things. In these circumstances you may want to simplify them and bring them up-to-date, perhaps based on the latest model articles. This is probably an excellent idea, but do not discard provisions that should be retained. Perhaps the founding fathers and founding mothers had good reasons for what they did and perhaps, in some instances at least, those reasons still hold.

PUTTING IN AN ARTICLE THAT DEFIES THE COMPANIES ACT OR SOME OTHER LAW

If this is done, the particular article will be ineffective. For example, the Companies Act 2006 prescribes minimum periods of notice for company meetings. Articles can make them longer but not shorter. If an article does attempt to make them shorter, it will be ineffective and the statutory minimum periods will apply.

MAKING A CHANGE NOT FOR THE BENEFIT OF THE COMPANY

A change must be for the benefit of the company and all its members and not for the benefit of just some of the members. This can be a very fine line and a matter of delicate judgment or, on the other hand, it can be glaringly obvious and a proposed change can amount to a fraud on the minority. If the line is crossed, there is a risk that a dissatisfied member may bring an action for unfair prejudice.

BUILDING IN AN INTERNAL CONTRADICTION

Something in your existing articles may contradict something in the model articles. If you adopt the model articles whilst retaining parts of your old articles, this may cause a problem.

A recent experience of mine is a very good example. I was asked to comment on a draft set of new articles prepared by an old-established company. They were proposing to adopt the model articles for private companies limited by shares, but subject to some additions and modifications. They had not excluded or modified Model Article 10 which includes '*In determining whether directors are participating in a directors' meeting, it is irrelevant where any director is or how they communicate with each other*'. An existing article, which they wished to retain, had been added. This excluded electronic directors' meetings and required directors' meetings to be held with directors in each others' presence.

MEMBERS' MEETINGS AND WRITTEN RESOLUTIONS

Annual general meetings

Annual general meetings remain compulsory for public companies. They are not held in private companies unless they are a specific requirement of the articles. Somewhat confusingly a reference to an AGM in the articles does not trigger the requirement. So, for example, a reference to directors retiring at the AGM does not require annual general meetings to be held. They will serve until they die, resign, become ineligible or are removed.

Neither the model articles for private companies nor the 1985 Table A for private companies require annual general meetings to be held. However, Reg. 47 of the 1948 Table A includes: '*The company shall each year hold a general meeting as its annual general meeting in addition to any other meetings in that year*'. If your company is regulated by the 1948 Table A, or if Reg. 47 of it is the default provision, AGMs are compulsory.

If your private company articles require AGMs to be held and you do not wish to do so, an appropriate amendment to the articles may be made. Similarly, but rather less probably, if you want to hold AGMs and they are not a requirement of the articles, an appropriate amendment may also be made.

Notice period for general meetings

CA2006 section 307 requires (other than for an adjourned meeting) the following minimum periods of notice to be given:

- 21 days for an AGM of a public company.
- 14 days for a general meeting of a public company.
- 14 days for an AGM (if held) or general meeting of a private company.

It is a recommendation of the UK Corporate Governance Code that listed companies give a minimum of 20 working days notice of all meetings.

The possibility of short notice is explained next in this chapter. The above periods are clear days. What this means can vary according to the articles and how the notice is given, but at least two days must be added (the day that the notice is sent and the day of the meeting) and probably more.

Articles cannot allow shorter notice than section 307 requires, but they can and frequently do require longer periods. If this is the case, it may be worth altering them to allow the statutory minimum periods. Directors can still choose to give longer periods if they wish.

Short notice of meetings

This section of the chapter relates to annual general meetings and general meetings, not board meetings.

Short notice of an annual general meeting of a public company is only permitted with the consent of all members entitled to attend and vote. Short notice of a general meeting of a public company is only permitted with the consent of the members who constitute a simple majority by number and 95 per cent by the nominal value of their shares. This was also the position under CA1985.

Short notice is permitted for all meetings of private companies, including AGMs, with the consent of members entitled to attend and vote who constitute a simple majority in number and 90 per cent by the nominal value of their shares. In the case of a company not having a share capital it is 90 per cent of the voting rights. Articles can increase the 90 per cent up to 95 per cent. Under the 1985 Act it was a simple majority and 95 per cent by value, unless an elective resolution reduced 95 per cent down to 90 per cent or any proportion between 90 per cent and 95 per cent.

Private companies having articles that specify a simple majority plus 95 per cent may wish to change them to take advantage of a simple majority plus 90 per cent.

It should be noted that short notice is not the same as no notice. Everyone must have a chance to attend.

Notice period for a special resolution

A special resolution may be passed as a written resolution in a private company, or at a meeting in a public company or a private company. If a special resolution is passed at a meeting, the period of notice for it is the same as the period of notice for the meeting, unless the articles specify a longer period. The minimum period of notice for the AGM of a public company is 21 days. The minimum period of notice for a general meeting of a public company or any meeting of a private company is 14 days. Articles may require longer than this.

The version of the 1985 Table A (Reg. 60) in force until 30th September 2007 requires 21 days notice to be given of a meeting at which a special resolution is to be proposed. The model articles and the version of Table A in force from 1st October 2007 to 30th September 2009 do not say that.

Companies regulated by the version of Table A in force until 30th September 2007 might consider changing their articles so that a special resolution can be passed after giving 14 days notice.

Proxies

CA1985 made the right of members to appoint a proxy to represent them at general meetings compulsory in all companies having a share capital. Furthermore, that Act gave minimum rights concerning proxies in these companies. Articles could give extra rights but could not reduce these minimum rights. The Act did not give members in a company limited by guarantee the right to appoint a proxy and if it was permitted by the articles, the rights were only what the articles specified.

CA2006 extended the compulsory rights and made them applicable in all companies, including companies limited by guarantee. Articles can give extra rights, though it is hard to think of any, but they cannot take away the statutory minimum. The rights include:

- Every member has a right to appoint a proxy of their choice.
- If there is a share capital, a member can appoint a proxy for each share.
- Proxies can attend, speak, vote on a show of hands, join in a demand for a poll and vote on a poll.

I recently advised a company whose articles endeavoured to restrict the members' choice of proxy. I had to tell the directors that this was not possible, something that they found hard to accept.

Many companies have articles purporting to restrict members' rights concerning proxies in ways contrary to the provisions of CA2006. These articles will be void and it is a good idea to remove them at a suitable opportunity.

Quorum at a members' meeting

CA2006 section 318 states that in a sole-member limited company the presence of one qualifying member at a meeting will constitute a quorum. This will take precedence over any higher number specified by the articles. Section 318 also states that in any other case two qualifying persons present at a meeting will constitute a quorum, but that this may be varied by any other number specified by the articles.

Articles do sometimes specify another number for a quorum and they do sometimes specify what must happen when a quorum is not present. Reg. 41 of Table A is as follows:

> *'If such a quorum is not present within half an hour from the time appointed for the meeting, or if during a meeting such a quorum ceases to be present, the meeting shall stand adjourned to the same day in the next week at the same time and place or to such time and place as the directors may determine.'*

The model articles say the same in slightly different words.

Setting the most appropriate number for a quorum is important and a delicate balance may need to be struck. There may be good reasons for a relatively high number but it can cause great difficulties. I have several times come across instances of the quorum being set too high and seen the resulting problems. I have seen several impassioned letters from the chairman imploring members to come to a meeting, and I have seen these backed up by the promise of splendid lunches and the chance to buy company products at special rates. No doubt a good time was had by all, but it should not be necessary.

Careful thought should be given to the matter and a suitable change should perhaps be considered. It may be sensible to include a provision that the number present (or a specified lower number) shall constitute a quorum at a duly convened adjourned meeting.

Voting on a show of hands and polls

All the model articles state that:

> *'A resolution put to the vote of a general meeting must be decided on a show of hands unless a poll is duly demanded in accordance with the articles'.*

Reg. 46 of Table A has the same effect.

The right to demand a poll cannot be excluded by the articles, other than on a resolution to elect the chairman of the meeting or adjourn the meeting. This is stipulated by CA2006 section 321. The same section specifies the minimum requirements for calling a poll. It states that a poll may be demanded:

> *'(a) by not less than 5 members having the right to vote on the resolution; or*
>
> *b) by a member or members representing not less than 10 per cent of the total voting rights of all the members having the right to vote on the resolution (excluding any voting rights attached to any shares in the company held as treasury shares); or*
>
> *c) by a member or members holding shares in the company conferring a right to vote on the resolution, being shares on which an aggregate sum has been paid up equal to not less than 10 per cent of the total sum paid up on all the shares conferring that right (excluding shares in the company conferring a right to vote on the resolution which are held as treasury shares).'*

Both the model articles and Table A do make it easier. The model articles state that a poll may be demanded in advance of the meeting, at the meeting before the vote on a show of hands or immediately after the declaration of the result of a vote on a show of hands, and that a poll may be demanded by:

- the chairman; or
- the directors; or
- two or more members who have the right to vote on the resolution; or
- a person or persons representing not less than one-tenth of the total voting rights of all the shareholders entitled to vote on the resolution.

Reg. 46 of Table A is the same, except that it does not allow the directors to demand a poll.

It is generally accepted that the chairman has a duty to demand a poll if he believes that the result would differ from the result of a vote on a show of hands.

It is unlikely that articles will make it more difficult to demand a poll than the provisions of section 321. If they do, they should be altered at a suitable opportunity. An increasing number of companies, especially listed companies, are dispensing with a show of hands and going straight to a poll on most or all resolutions. It saves time and everyone knows that a poll will be held. On the other hand it may be useful to know the headcount opinion on the day. This is my view but many people think differently. It is something that should perhaps be considered.

Chairman of a general meeting and the chairman's casting vote

Who chairs a general meeting? Regs. 42 and 43 of Table A are as follows:

> '42. *The chairman, if any, of the board of directors or in his absence some other director nominated by the directors shall preside as chairman of the meeting, but if neither the chairman nor such other director (if any) be present within fifteen minutes after the time appointed for holding the meeting and willing to act, the directors present shall elect one of their number to be chairman and, if there is only one director present and willing to act, he shall be chairman.*

> 43. *If no director is willing to act as chairman, or if no director is present within fifteen minutes after the time appointed for holding the meeting, the members present and entitled to vote shall choose one of their number to be chairman.'*

The model articles are very similar but not quite identical. Article 39 in the model articles for private companies limited by shares is as follows:

> '(1) *If the directors have appointed a chairman, the chairman shall chair general meetings if present and willing to do so.*
>
> (2) *If the directors have not appointed a chairman, or if the chairman is unwilling to chair the meeting or is not present within ten minutes of the time at which a meeting was due to start:*
>
> a) the directors present, or
>
> b) (if no directors are present), the meeting,
>
> *must appoint a director or shareholder to chair the meeting, and the appointment of the chairman of the meeting must be the first business of the meeting.*
>
> (3) *The person chairing a meeting in accordance with this article is referred to as "the chairman of the meeting".'*

Other articles may make different arrangements. If your articles do not reflect the wishes of the members, a change should be considered.

Table A for companies incorporated up to 30th September 2007 gives the chairman a casting vote, which may be exercised in addition to any other votes that he may have. Neither Table A for companies incorporated from 1st October 2007 nor the new model articles give the chairman a casting vote. It is not permitted for the chairman of a traded company to have a casting vote but, in other companies, it is permitted if the articles allow it. It is thought that in a company incorporated on or after 1st October 2007 the chairman may only have a casting vote if he is a member.

Written resolutions of the members

This section of the chapter relates to written resolutions of members, not written resolutions of directors.

Written resolutions of the members in a public company are not permitted, but they are permitted in all private companies and they cannot be prohibited by the articles. Furthermore minimum rights are guaranteed by CA2006. Articles may add to these rights but may not reduce or remove them. Written resolutions are very popular in private companies, and in many of them they are in practice the main or exclusive way that business is conducted.

CA2006 is much more detailed and prescriptive than CA1985 in this matter. Many companies have procedures specified in their articles that are no longer required or, in some cases, no longer permitted. A suitable opportunity should be taken to remove them.

One point in particular merits attention. CA2006 specifies that a written resolution will lapse after 28 days if the required number of signatures have not been delivered to the company. This 28 day time limit may be varied by the articles and you might prefer a longer or, perhaps more probably, shorter period.

DIRECTORS

Directors' meetings

Like Table A, the model articles do not specify the period of notice that must be given for a board meeting. In *Browne v La Trinidad 1887* it was established that reasonable notice must be given and that what is reasonable depends on individual circumstances. In this particular case five minutes notice was held to be reasonable. Quite a few companies' articles specify minimum periods of notice, sometimes relatively lengthy periods, and these may or may not still be deemed appropriate.

The model articles allow directors to waive their right to receive notice and to do so up to seven days after the meeting has been held. This is not in Table A and could be useful if there has been an inadvertent failure to inform a director that a meeting will be held. Table A does not require notice to be given to a director who is not in the United Kingdom. This is not in the model articles, which seems sensible given the modern ease of communications.

All the model articles contain the following:

> '(1) *Subject to the articles, directors participate in a directors' meeting, or part of a directors' meeting, when:*
>
> a) *the meeting has been called and takes place in accordance with the articles, and*
>
> b) *they can each communicate to the others any information or opinions they have on any particular item of the business of the meeting.*
>
> (2) *In determining whether directors are participating in a directors' meeting, it is irrelevant where any director is or how they communicate with each other.*
>
> (3) *If all the directors participating in a meeting are not in the same place, they may decide that the meeting is to be treated as taking place wherever any of them is.'*

It is article 10 in the private company model articles and article 9 in the public company model articles. Electronic meetings were already relatively common, but this specifically legitimises them and many companies will wish to adopt this article or something similar. A word of warning – this legitimises an electronic meeting where all participants have real time communication – a conference telephone call for example. It is not clear that it legitimises something that does not meet this standard – a series of telephone calls with the chairman relaying points of view for example.

Alternate directors

Alternate directors are only possible if provision is made for them in the articles. There is provision in Table A and the model articles for public companies, though the details are not the same. There is no provision for alternate directors in the model articles for private companies.

If your articles do not provide for the possible appointment of alternate directors and if you wish them to do so, you may insert suitable provision. It may be sensible to use the appropriate articles from the model articles for public companies, but you can use the appropriate regulations from Table A or some other wording if you wish.

Minimum and maximum number of directors

CA2006 (like CA1985) requires public companies to have at least two directors. Both Acts permit private companies to have a sole director if this is permitted by the articles. Neither Act imposes a maximum number of directors, though the articles may do so. It is a legal requirement that all companies have at least one director who is a 'natural person'. This means a human being as opposed to a corporate director.

None of the model articles impose a minimum or maximum number. Table A imposes no maximum number, but it does stipulate a minimum of two unless the members determine otherwise by means of an ordinary resolution. A private company having a sole director and relying on Table A is running a risk. If the number of directors is below the required minimum, Table A only allows the directors to meet to call a general meeting at which additional directors may be appointed or (if it is allowed by the articles) to appoint additional directors themselves. If they act beyond these limitations, they are exceeding their powers. This situation may be, to say the least, highly inconvenient.

It is a good idea that the articles of a private company should permit a sole director, or at least a realistic minimum number. It may also be sensible to ensure that remaining directors can continue to act, notwithstanding that their number has fallen below a specified minimum.

Removal and termination of directors

CA2006 section 168 gives members the right to remove a director by means of an ordinary resolution. This right cannot be taken away by the articles or a service contract with the director and members must receive special notice of the resolution. Members may remove a director at an annual general meeting or at a general meeting. The decision must be made by a simple majority of those voting. The director concerned must be given notice of the resolution. He may make written representations in advance of the meeting and this may be done at the company's expense. He may also attend the meeting and speak at it. Articles may not make it more difficult than this. Removal by the members cannot be done by means of a written resolution.

Apart from this, appointment terminates on death, due to a process of law or in accordance with the articles. Retirement by rotation is dealt with next in this chapter. All the model articles are the same concerning termination and state:

'A person ceases to be a director as soon as:

- *a) that person ceases to be a director by virtue of any provision of the Companies Act 2006 or is prohibited from being a director by law;*
- *b) a bankruptcy order is made against that person;*
- *c) a composition is made with that person's creditors generally in satisfaction of that person's debts;*
- *d) a registered medical practitioner who is treating that person gives a written opinion to the company stating that that person has become physically or mentally incapable of acting as a director and may remain so for more than three months;*
- *e) by reason of that person's mental health, a court makes an order which wholly or partly prevents that person from personally exercising any powers or rights which that person would otherwise have;*
- *f) notification is received by the company from the director that the director is resigning or retiring from office, and such resignation or retirement has taken effect in accordance with its terms.'*

This has many similarities with Reg. 81 of Table A but there are some differences. In particular Table A, but not the model articles, states *'he shall for more than six months have been absent without permission of the directors from meetings of directors held during that period and the directors resolve that his office be vacated.'* This has always struck me as unreasonable because the frequency of board meetings varies so much in different companies. At a company having weekly meetings a director can miss 25 out of 26 and be safe, but at a company having two board meetings a year a director's train can be cancelled and he may be vulnerable.

Many companies vary the provisions of the model articles and there are hundreds of possibilities. It might, for example, be appropriate to include failure to hold a particular professional qualification or failure to own a specified number of the company's shares.

Neither the model articles nor table A enable the directors to remove a director, other than because of 'absent without permission' as provided for by Table A. Numerous companies' articles do allow the directors to remove a director and, if your articles do not provide for this, it is something that should perhaps be considered.

Retirement of directors by rotation

Both Table A and the model articles for public companies require the directors to retire by rotation. However, the way that this operates is different and simpler under the model articles. If the articles call for retirement by rotation and this is not wanted, the detailed provisions should be removed from the articles. Similarly if it is wished that retirement by rotation should operate in a way different from the current requirement, the articles should be changed.

The model articles do not require directors of private companies to retire by rotation. The effect is that directors serve until they die, resign, become ineligible or are removed. The 1985 Table A refers to directors retiring by rotation at the annual general meeting but does not explicitly require annual general meetings to be held. The effect is that directors do not retire and serve until they die, resign, become ineligible or are removed. The 1948 Table A refers to directors retiring at the annual general meeting and does explicitly require annual general meetings to be held. This means that directors do retire by rotation and the same may be the case in specially drafted articles. If your articles do not reflect your wishes, they may be changed.

Chairman of directors' meetings and the chairman's casting vote

Subject to the articles the directors may elect a chairman for an indefinite period or for a fixed term. They may decide to rotate the chairmanship or elect a chairman just for one meeting. They may decide to operate without a chairman, though this is unusual. If Table A or the new model articles apply, the chairman, in addition to his normal vote, will have a casting vote. It should be noted that there is no inherent right to a casting vote. There will only be a casting vote if the articles provide for one.

Directors' duty to avoid conflicts of interest (CA2006 section 175)

CA2006 section 175 requires a director of a company to '*avoid a situation in which he has, or can have, a direct or indirect interest that conflicts, or possibly may conflict, with the interest of the company*'. It does not apply to a conflict of interest arising in relation to a transaction or arrangement with the company, or if the situation cannot reasonably be regarded as likely to give rise to a conflict of interest. Subject to conditions a conflict can be authorised by the members and subject to conditions it may be authorised by the directors. Authorisation by the directors is possible if:

- In the case of a public company authorisation is permitted by the constitution.
- In the case of a private company registered before 1st October 2008 authorisation is permitted by the constitution.
- In the case of a private company registered on or after 1st October 2008 authorisation is not prohibited by the constitution.

It is probable that most companies would wish their directors to be able to authorise a conflict of interest. Table A does not provide the necessary authority. Virtually all listed companies and many other companies have made an appropriate change to their constitution. If it is not permitted in your company, it is something that should be considered. Of course if it is permitted and it is not wanted, it can be prohibited in the articles or by means of a special resolution.

Directors' duty to declare interest in proposed transaction or arrangement (CA2006 section 177)

CA2006 section 177 relates to an interest that a director has in a proposed transaction or arrangement with the company. This is distinct from the duty to avoid conflicts of interest (section 175). Under section 177 directors are required to disclose to the directors details of any interest they have in a proposed transaction or arrangement with the company. There are certain exceptions listed in section 177.

The model articles stipulate that, with certain exceptions, an interested director cannot be counted in a quorum or vote on a matter in which he has declared an interest. This may be considered inconvenient and undesirable, especially where there are a small number of directors and it may be difficult to obtain a quorum. The same difficulty may obtain if there are a large number of directors and many of them have the same interest. It is possible to insert into the articles provisions that allow a director who has declared an interest in accordance with section 177 to participate in the meeting.

It is worth mentioning that under section 172 *'A director of a company must act in the way he considers, in good faith, would be most likely to promote the success of the company for the benefit of its members as a whole.'* If a director does participate in a meeting having declared an interest in proposed transaction or arrangement, he should keep this in mind.

Directors' indemnity

CA2006 goes further than CA1985 in permitting, but not of course requiring, companies to indemnify their directors against certain risks. Companies were already permitted to fund a director's defence costs in court proceedings, and this has been extended to regulatory proceedings and also to associated companies. In addition companies are now permitted to indemnify directors against liability incurred in connection with the company's activity as trustee of a pension scheme, where the company is trustee of an occupational pension scheme. This too extends to associated companies.

The model articles provide these extra indemnities (it is article 38 in the model articles for private companies limited by shares) but Table A does not. If your articles do not provide these extra indemnities, you may wish to change them so that they do. Some companies endeavour to go further than the general provisions in the model articles and give specific details of what may be done.

SHARE CAPITAL AND SHARES

Authorised share capital

Since 1st October 2009 there has been no requirement for a company to have authorised share capital. The concept only exists in the company if there is provision for it in the constitution. There is no such provision in the model articles. There is also no such provision in Table A, but this is because until 1st October 2009 it was a compulsory component of the memorandum. On 1st October 2009 the authorised share capital specified in the memorandum was deemed to be part of the articles.

Most people believe that authorised share capital had little purpose, which is why it is no longer compulsory. If it is part of your articles, you may well want to take it out. At the very least this will shorten the note about share capital in the statutory accounts. It takes an ordinary resolution to remove authorised share capital from the articles. This is an exception to the general rule that almost all changes to the constitution require a special resolution.

Partly paid shares

Partly paid shares are now much less common than was formerly the case. They are permitted by Table A and by the model articles for public companies, but they are not permitted by the model articles for private companies limited by shares.

If the issue of partly paid shares is wished or if the option of doing so is desired, and if it is not permitted by the articles, suitable changes must be made.

Allotment of shares

Under CA1985 shares could be allotted by the directors provided that either the articles or an ordinary resolution of the members allowed them to do so. The authority of the directors to allow shares could not exceed five years unless, in a private company only, there was an elective resolution to give them indefinite authority.

Under CA2006 the position is the same for public companies and for private companies that will have more than one class of share after the allotment. However, an elective resolution in a private company passed before 1st October 2008 allowing directors indefinite authority to allow shares, continues to allow them to do so.

The position is different for private companies that will only have one class of share after the allotment. Directors in these companies have indefinite authority to allot shares unless this authority is restricted by the company's articles.

If it is wished to restrict the authority of the directors of a private company to allot shares and if the articles do not do so, it is necessary to change the articles.

Purchase of own shares

Companies may purchase their own shares, subject to conditions and procedures, provided that the shares are fully paid and provided that it is not prohibited by the articles. This differs from the position under CA1985, which was that the articles had to give authority. The 1985 Table A does give authority and the model articles for both public and private companies are silent on the point, which is sufficient.

Redeemable shares

Public companies may issue redeemable shares if it is permitted by their articles. Private companies may issue redeemable shares so long as it is not prohibited by their articles. In both cases this may only be done if irredeemable shares are in issue.

Transfer of shares

Shares are freely transferable unless the articles place restrictions on transferability. Table A and the model articles for public companies only give directors discretion to refuse a transfer if the shares are not fully paid. The model articles for private companies limited by shares, on the other hand, give directors discretion to refuse a transfer of fully paid shares. The articles of private companies frequently impose restrictions on the transfer of shares. There are numerous possibilities but three commonly encountered are:

- Directors are given discretion to refuse a transfer.
- Articles require that the transferee conforms with certain conditions. This could be, for example, that the transferee holds a specified professional qualification.
- Shares must first be offered to existing shareholders pro rata to their holding. Only if they refuse the opportunity to buy the shares at the price agreed by the proposed transferee may the transfer proceed.

One of the directors' general duties (CA1985 section 172) is to act in a way that they consider, in good faith, would be most likely to promote the success of the company for the benefit of its members as a whole. This means that they should exercise any discretion given to them in the interests of the company and its members as a whole, and not, for example, refuse a share transfer just because they do not like the proposed transferee.

If articles place restrictions on the transfer of shares and if it is intended that the restrictions should remain, care should be taken to retain them if the articles are changed. There is, though, one thing that may well be different. CA2006 requires that if directors intend to refuse to accept a transfer of shares, they must communicate their decision and the reasons for it as soon as practicable, but in any case within two months. They must answer reasonable questions about their motives, but they cannot be compelled to divulge board minutes. Articles sometimes say that directors may refuse to transfer shares and need not disclose their reasons. This is now overridden by CA2006 section 771 and any such provision in the articles should be removed at a convenient opportunity.

OTHER MATTERS

Provision for the death of all the directors and members

Numerous small private companies have a small number of directors who own all the shares, perhaps just a sole director who owns all the shares. The death of this person or persons can cause great difficulties for the company, family members etc. Provision for this eventuality is made in article 17 of the private company model articles. This, in part, reads as follows:

> '(2) *In any case where, as a result of death, the company has no members and no directors, the personal representatives of the last member to have died have the right, by notice in writing, to appoint a person to be a director.*
>
> (3) *For the purposes of paragraph (2), where 2 or more members die in circumstances rendering it uncertain who was the last to die, a younger member is deemed to have survived an older member.'*

A similar article is in the model articles for private companies limited by guarantee.

This is not in Table A and if it is not in your articles, it is well worth incorporating it.

Age and other discrimination

There was formerly a statutory upper age limit of 70 for directors of public companies and for directors of private companies that were subsidiaries of public companies. Directors of such companies were required to come off the board at the AGM following their 70th birthday. They could offer themselves for re-election and then, having had special notice of the director's date of birth, it was up to the shareholders. Subsequent re-elections and the new appointment of an over-age director were also the subject of special notice to the shareholders. Shareholders could therefore decide to have directors over the age of 70. There were no such restrictions in other companies.

Statutory restrictions relating to an upper age limit for directors have now been removed. CA2006 specifies a minimum age of 16 for directors and requires all companies to have at least one director who is a 'natural person', as opposed to a corporate director.

Some companies incorporated age limits for directors in their articles and a very few companies may have incorporated unacceptable other forms of discrimination. Such discrimination, if it is present, contravenes the Equality Act 2010 and serious thought should be given to having it removed. Under this Act unlawful discrimination may relate to:

- Age
- Disability
- Gender reassignment
- Marriage and civil partnership
- Pregnancy and maternity
- Race
- Religion or belief
- Sex
- Sexual orientation

Objects

This subject is comprehensively covered in Chapter 3 and it is not necessary to do so again here.

Electronic and website communication with members

Subject to conditions, companies are permitted to communicate with their members electronically, by e-mail or by website. This can cover notices of meetings, communication of proxy notices, provision of statutory accounts and other things. There are obvious cost and other benefits for companies with a significant membership.

It is permissible for a company to send documents electronically to a member who has agreed to accept documents by e-mail and supplied an e-mail address for this purpose. Companies are not compelled to communicate electronically and each individual member retains the right to require communication in paper form. A quoted company must be authorised by a resolution of the members or by its articles to communicate by e-mail in this way. A resolution of the members is not required in unquoted companies.

All companies are allowed, but not compelled, to communicate with members by placing information on a website. In the case of all companies, not just quoted companies, this can only be done if it is authorised by the articles or by a resolution of the members. Members must be asked for their agreement individually and they may not be asked more frequently than once a year. Failure to respond within 28 days may be taken by the company as agreement. Each member has the individual right to withhold agreement, to withdraw agreement and to insist on paper in a particular case. In respect of website communication to a member who has given agreement, the company must notify the member each time something is placed on the website. This notification may be delivered electronically or by post.

All the model articles permit communication as described above. If you wish to take advantage of website communication and it is not authorised by the articles, a suitable change will be required.

Failure to notify contact details

This is Article 80 in the model articles for public companies. Losing contact with a member or members can be a headache. Sometimes the shareholding is trivial or, in a company limited by guarantee, the 'lost' members may be a small part of a large membership. This article could help. It is not in Table A and it is not in the model articles for private companies.

A Thorogood Special Briefing

Chapter 6
How articles and the company name are changed

- Introduction
- A piece of advice
- Another piece of advice
- The way that articles are changed
- Considerations for listed companies
- Variation in class rights
- Change of company name
- Example of special resolution to alter articles
- Example of special resolution to adopt new articles
- Example of special resolution for change of name of company
- Example of written special resolution to alter articles
- Example of certified copy of written special resolution for Companies House

Chapter 6
How articles and the company name are changed

Introduction

The previous chapter posed the question of whether the articles should be changed and detailed some of the issues that might well be considered. This chapter moves beyond the question and explains in detail how articles are changed and also how the name of the company is changed. The latter part of the chapter provides some specimen resolutions and gives an example of a suitable certified copy for Companies House.

This chapter proceeds on the assumption that it is the company that initiates the change. It should though be mentioned that although it is rare, both a change in the articles and a change of name may be imposed on the company. The court can impose a change of articles when dealing with an action for unfair prejudice brought under CA2006 section 994. The Secretary of State can require a company to change its name if there has been a successful objection to the name of the company.

Finally, it should be mentioned that the constitution (including the articles and the company name) are 'owned' by the members. It follows that only the members can make changes. The directors cannot do so, though they frequently propose changes to the members. If the directors are the members they make the decision in their capacity as members. It seems obvious but it is misunderstood surprisingly often.

A piece of advice

It may be possible to achieve a desired change to the constitution just by means of a resolution, rather than by a resolution that changes the articles. This can seem attractive because it saves the job of reprinting the articles. This will have the consequence of making the constitution harder to follow in the future, perhaps only slightly harder but much harder if there are many changes over a significant period. Future directors, company secretaries, members, others and possibly even yourself, if you are forgetful, would appreciate being able to see it all in one convenient place. It is probably worth changing the articles.

Another piece of advice

When the articles are changed the amended version must be reprinted, and at the very least registered at Companies House. If the articles are long, it may be a significant job to have them retyped. This is why it is worth keeping a set of articles electronically, and if the preparation and printing has been done by an adviser such as a solicitor, making sure that you get a copy. It may be a simple job to amend the electronic version.

The way that articles are changed

Articles must be printed and divided into consecutively numbered paragraphs.

The minimum requirement to change the articles is a special resolution, but if the articles are entrenched, a majority higher than that required for a special resolution is necessary. Entrenchment is explained in Chapter 4. It is not possible to change the articles by a vote less demanding than a special resolution.

A special resolution to change the articles, either at a meeting or (in a private company) by a written resolution, may be requisitioned by the members. However, it is much more frequently proposed to the members, either at a meeting or (in a private company) by a written resolution by the directors. It is normal (but not a requirement) that the directors send a letter or circular explaining the resolution and their reasons for wishing it to be passed and in many cases notify members how and where the proposed new articles may be inspected.

The resolution is voted upon. If this is done at a meeting, the resolution must (subject to obtaining a quorum and the possibility of entrenchment) receive 75 per cent of the votes cast. If it is a written resolution, it must (subject to the possibility of entrenchment) receive 75 per cent of the votes that could be passed.

If the special resolution is passed, a certified copy must be sent to Companies House within 15 days. This is normally signed by the chairman of the meeting, but it may be signed by any director or the company secretary. If new articles have been adopted, a certified copy must be filed at Companies House with the resolution. This must also be done if there has been a significant alteration to the articles. If the amendment is a minor and obvious textual one, a neatly altered copy of the articles may be sent instead of a new set of articles.

A change to the company's objects (addition to, removal of or alteration to) must be notified to Companies House on form CC04. This is in addition to a copy of the resolution and a copy of the new or revised articles. The change to the objects does not take effect until this form has been registered by Companies House. Form CC04 is not required for any other change to the articles. If the resolution entrenches the articles form CC01 must be submitted to Companies House and if it ends entrenchment form CC02 must be submitted. If existing entrenchment is varied but not cancelled form CC03 must be submitted.

If Companies House becomes aware that articles have been altered and a new or revised set of articles has not been submitted to it, it may serve a notice on the company requiring articles to be delivered. Failure to do so within the specified period will result in a civil penalty on the company of £200. Regardless of this, failure to deliver a certified copy of the resolution and the new or amended articles to Companies House within 15 days is an offence committed by the company and every officer in default. In practice prosecutions are rare.

Considerations for listed companies

Listed companies are not required to obtain advance approval from the UK Listing Authority for a proposed change to their articles. They may, though, choose to consult the UKLA, especially if any of the proposed changes are controversial or unusual. They must send a copy of the draft amendments to any regulated market on which the company's securities are issued and also to the FSA. This must be done no later than the date of calling the general meeting at which the change is to be proposed.

Listed companies are also required to send a circular to their shareholders. This must explain the proposed changes and either give the full terms of the proposed amendments or state where they may be inspected. Two copies of the circular must be lodged with the Document Viewing Facility and a Regulatory Information Service must be informed that this has been done.

When (and if) the proposed amendment has been passed the Regulatory Information Service must be informed of this fact and two copies of the resolution must be lodged with the Document Viewing Facility.

Variation in class rights

CA2006 gives some protection to members holding a class of shares who are adversely affected by a change in the articles. Section 633 permits the holders of not less in the aggregate than 15 per cent of the class in question to apply to the court to have the variation in the articles cancelled. The application to the court must be made within 21 days of the passing of the resolution and the applicants must not have consented to or voted for the change. The court has the power to disallow the variation in class rights.

There is also provision to apply to the court in respect of variation in class rights in a company not having a share capital.

Change of company name

A company name may always be changed by a special resolution. It may also be changed by a procedure specified in its articles. There are many possibilities for this but the most common is probably a decision of the directors.

The change of name does not take effect until the Registrar issues a certificate of incorporation on change of name. The company's registered number does not change. A certified copy of the special resolution (if there has been a special resolution) must be submitted to Companies House. One of the following must also be submitted:

- NM01 Notice of change of name by resolution
- NM02 Notice of change of name by conditional resolution
- NM04 Notice of change of name by means provided for in the articles
- NM05 Notice of change of name by resolution of directors

A fee of £10 is payable (£50 for same day service). If form NM02 is submitted, the name is protected. Form NM03 (Notice confirming satisfaction of the conditional resolution for change of name) must be submitted when the condition is satisfied and the change of name is to proceed.

When the certificate of incorporation on change of name is issued the company's name must be altered on company notepaper and certain other documents (including forms of electronic communication), on the company seal (if there is one), and outside the registered office and other company offices. A copy of the special resolution (if applicable) and a copy of the Registrar's certificate should be attached to copies of the articles held by the company, and express references to the company's name in the articles should be annotated to indicate the change of name. It is not necessary to send a revised copy of the articles to Companies House.

The restrictions on a permissible choice of company name are the same as those when a new company is registered. The whole subject is comprehensively explained in Companies House guidance booklet GP1 which may be obtained from Companies House website **www.companieshouse.gov.uk**. This gives more information than the following (including a list of the words for which permission is required) and is recommended reading. The following is an abbreviated summary:

The correct ending must be used

If the company is a private limited company the name must end with 'Limited' or 'Ltd', or if it is registered in Wales, the Welsh language equivalents. This is with the exception of private companies limited by guarantee that fulfil certain criteria and have successfully applied for exemption.

If the company is a public company the name must end with 'Public Limited Company' or 'PLC', or if it is registered in Wales, the Welsh language equivalents.

These words must only be used at the end of the name.

The name must not be the 'same as' the name of a company already registered

Companies House will reject an application if an existing company already has the name. This was once an extremely difficult job for the staff but it is now easily accomplished by computers. There are various rules about acceptable and unacceptable minor differences. For example & is treated the same as 'and'. 'Hand-S Limited' would be rejected if 'Hands Ltd' was already registered.

The name must not in the opinion of the Secretary of State constitute a criminal offence

For example, the name must not indicate that the company is a bank unless it is recognised as such by the Bank of England.

The name must not in the opinion of the Secretary of State be offensive

This is intended for family reading so no examples will be given, but certain Anglo-Saxon four letter words are unlikely to be acceptable.

The name must not in the opinion of the Secretary of State suggest a connection with national or local government, or a devolved administration or certain specified public authorities

Such a name may only be registered with the permission of the Secretary of State.

The name contains words for which appropriate permission must be obtained and this has not happened

There is a list of words that may only be used with appropriate permission. For example, 'Police' may only be used for an England and Wales company with the permission of the Home Office. 'Dentist' may only be used with the permission of the General Dental Council.

It is interesting to note that until recently the place name 'Sheffield' was protected in this way. This was because of the once-mighty steel industry associated with the city. Other cities and towns did not have similar concessions and one speculates about the extent of the lobbying that must have been necessary to obtain it.

Example of special resolution to alter articles

THAT the articles of association of the company be altered as follows:

a) by deleting in article .... the words ....

b) by substituting for the existing article .... the following article

....; and

c) by deleting in article .... the words ....

And substituting therefor the words ....

Example of special resolution to adopt new articles

THAT the regulations contained in the document submitted to this meeting and, for the purpose of identification, signed by the chairman hereof be approved and adopted as the articles of association of the company in substitution for and to the exclusion of all the existing articles thereof.

Example of special resolution for change of name of company

THAT the name of the company be changed to

....Limited/Public Limited Company

Example of written special resolution to alter articles

Company Number ....

Written Special Resolution of ....**Limited**

Circulation Date...

Pursuant to chapter 2 of Part 13 of the Companies Act 2006 the members of the company resolve that the resolution set out below be passed as a special resolution of the company.

'THAT the articles of association of the company be altered as follows:

a) by deleting in article .... the words ....

b) by substituting for the existing article .... the following article

.....................; and

c) by deleting in article .... The words ....

and substituting therefor the words ....'

Please read through the notes at the end of this document before signifying your agreement to the resolution.

We being members entitled to vote at a general meeting of the company hereby agree to the resolution

Signed

.... Date ....

.... Date ....

Notes

1. If you agree with the Resolutions please indicate your agreement by signing and dating this document where indicated above and returning it to the Company.
2. Once you have indicated your agreement to the Resolutions you may not revoke your agreement.
3. If you do not agree to the resolutions, you do not need to do anything. You will not be deemed to agree if you fail to reply.
4. Unless within the period of 28 days beginning with the Circulation Date sufficient agreement has been received to pass the Resolutions, they will lapse. If you agree to the Resolutions please ensure that your agreement reaches us before or during that date.

Writer's footnotes

1. *Written resolutions are not available to public companies.*
2. *The members may sign a single document or several documents with identical words.*
3. *the response period is automatically 28 days unless varied by the company's articles.*

Example of certified copy of written special resolution for Companies House

Company Number ....

RESOLUTION

OF

... LIMITED

On .... The following special resolution was duly passed as a written resolution in accordance with the requirements of sections 288 to 300 of the Companies Act 2006 by the requisite majority of the members of the company.

'THAT the articles of association of the company be altered as follows:

a) by deleting in article .... the words ....

b) by substituting for the existing article .... the following article ....; and

c) by deleting in article .... the words .... and substituting therefor the words ....

....

DIRECTOR/SECRETARY

A Thorogood Special Briefing

Chapter 7

Review of model articles for private companies

- Introduction
- Liability of members (Article 2)
- Directors' powers and responsibilities (Articles 3-6)
- Decision making by directors (Articles 7-16)
- Appointment of directors (Articles 17-20)
- Shares (Articles 21-29)
- Dividends and other distributions (Articles 30-35)
- Capitalisation of profits (Article 36)
- Organisation of general meetings (Articles 37-41)
- Voting at general meetings (Articles 42-47)
- Administrative arrangements (Articles 48-51)
- Directors' indemnity and insurance (Articles 52-53)
- Model articles for private companies limited by guarantee

Chapter 7
Review of model articles for private companies

Introduction

Around 99.7 per cent of companies registered at Companies House are private companies. Of these the overwhelming majority (more than 96 per cent) are private companies limited by shares, with the others being limited by guarantee. Despite the size and importance of the other 0.3 per cent of companies it is the private company model articles that receive the most attention and are likely to be significant to most readers.

Almost all of this chapter consists of an article by article review of the model articles for private companies limited by shares. It follows the order of the model articles which differs from the order used in Table A. The new order is said to be more logical. As well as focusing on important points the chapter draws attention to similarities with and differences from Table A. The model articles are significantly shorter and simpler than Table A. The following elements of Table A do not feature at all.

- Making calls on shares or for liens or forfeiture of shares if a call is not paid.
- Retirement of directors by rotation.
- Retirement of directors following their initial appointment.
- The possibility of alternate directors.
- Disposing of fractions of shares on a consolidation.
- Appointment and removal of a company secretary, if there is one.
- Uncertificated shares or share warrants.

The model articles for private companies limited by guarantee are virtually identical to the model articles for private companies limited by shares, though of course the article numbers are different and there is no mention of shares and dividends. They have a small section at the end of the chapter.

Liability of members (Article 2)

The article establishes the limited liability of the members. This is vital and should on no account be omitted if stand-alone articles are registered or if the articles are altered. There is no corresponding article in Table A because it was formerly a matter for the memorandum.

Directors' powers and responsibilities (Articles 3-6)

This section of the model articles gives directors the power to run the company. It is, in general, close to Table A but the power to delegate is more extensive and more explicit.

Article 3 – Directors' general authority

This article gives the directors the full authority that they need to manage the company's business, subject to the reserve power of the shareholders (Article 4). It is generally accepted that the directors need this authority and this article, but it is possible to limit the authority in various ways. It is subject to the articles but the model articles place no restriction. Article 3 has the same effect as the more wordy Reg. 70 of Table A.

Article 4 – Shareholders' reserve power

Shareholders only have this reserve power if it is provided by the articles. Any use of it by the shareholders must be lawful and cannot have backdated effect.

Article 5 – Directors may delegate

Some delegation is essential in all but very small companies. Without it the business of the company would not be possible. This article goes further than Regs. 71 and 72 of Table A. The power to delegate is very wide and includes the power to delegate to persons who are not directors. The person or committee to whom delegation has been made may be authorised to delegate further. Of course some things may not be delegated. Signing the balance sheet and signing a declaration of solvency are two examples.

Article 6 – Committees

This requires committees to follow the rules applying to directors as far as they are applicable, and permits directors to make further rules for them. It is effectively the same as part of Reg. 72 of Table A.

Decision making by directors (Articles 7-16)

We all know that in many companies directors ignore the articles in this very important area. Indeed many directors have no idea what rules the articles establish. This is particularly the case in small, owner-managed companies. With this in mind these articles relax the Table A requirements and legitimise what already happened in many companies. This relaxation has been generally welcomed.

Article 7 – Directors to take decisions collectively

If a decision is taken at a meeting as opposed to a unanimous decision without a meeting, it is one director one vote and the majority decides. It is possible for articles to give more power to some directors or sections of directors, but the model articles do not do so. Directors have equal powers. Of course we know that in some companies, as George Orwell might have put it, some directors are more equal than others. If so, it is what the directors want or accept, not what this article says.

Article 7 also makes clear that if there is only one director and the articles do not require there to be more than one director, there is no need for formality in decision making. Table A does not make this explicit.

Article 8 – Unanimous decisions

This is based on Reg. 93 of Table A, though Reg. 93 mentions alternate directors. 'Unanimous' is defined as all eligible directors able to vote on a matter, whereas Table A defines it as all directors entitled to receive notice of a meeting. It is made clear that a decision may be communicated in any manner and not just in writing. This can include e-mail for example, or even a series of telephone calls to the chairman or company secretary.

Article 9 – Calling a directors' meeting

This corresponds with part of Reg. 88 of Table A. Like Reg. 88 it provides that any director may call a meeting or have a meeting called. There are, though, some important new and additional points:

- Notice must include the proposed date, place and time.
- Details of how directors will communicate with each other if they are not in the same place, must be specified.
- The right of directors to waive notice.

Reg. 88 states that it is not necessary to give notice to a director who is not in the UK. This is not in the model articles. It is possibly omitted because the enormous advance of electronic communication has made it much easier for directors not in the UK to keep in touch. Also, the new model articles make it easy (and probably common) for directors to hold meetings without being in the same place, or even on the same continent.

Article 10 – Participation in directors' meetings

This article has received a lot of attention and goes beyond the provisions of Table A. Subject to conditions *'it is irrelevant where any director is or how they communicate with each other'*. This permits telephone board meetings, video conference board meetings and real-time e-mail communication. It is suggested that some form of simultaneous communication is essential and that the article does not cover a chairman relaying the substance of telephone calls or exchanges of e-mails over a period. It is possible that in due course case law will clarify the limits of what is permitted.

The article includes, which Table A does not, *'If all the directors participating in a meeting are not in the same place, they may decide that the meeting is to be treated as taking place wherever one of them is'*. This means that five directors could be in England and one sipping cocktails on the beach in an exotic tax haven, and a board meeting is being held in the tax haven. In some companies it is important to show that control is exercised in a particular jurisdiction, and this could have important tax implications. However, your writer, though not a tax expert, suspects that the tax authorities will not lightly accept this resulting in a reduction of tax payable. An unwelcome consequence (for some) could be that directors have fewer reasons for spending time in tax havens.

Article 11 – Quorum for directors' meeting

The directors themselves may fix the number for a quorum, but in the absence of a decision it is two. This is the same as Reg. 89 of Table A, though this mentions alternate directors. If the total number of directors is less than the number required for a quorum, the continuing directors can only act to appoint further directors (which is permitted by the model articles) or to call a general meeting so that the shareholders can appoint further directors. Difficulties in obtaining a quorum or even the impossibility of doing so can cause great difficulties and companies are well advised to specify a realistic number in their articles. If the articles do not specify a number, the directors would be well advised to make a realistic provision and minute their decision. It can of course be a fine judgment. A tiny coterie of directors should not be able to railroad the board, perhaps in the holiday season.

Article 12 – Chairing of directors' meetings

This is close to Reg. 91 of Table A but there are a couple of subtle differences. As in Reg. 91 the directors may appoint a chairman, but unlike Reg. 91 they must (not may) appoint a replacement if the chairman does not participate. They must do this after five minutes after the appointed time, rather than the ten minutes specified by Reg. 91. There is no statutory requirement that the directors appoint a chair or that the articles permit it. Most boards do appoint a chair, but some do not.

Article 13 – Casting vote

As with Reg. 88 of Table A, the chairman has a casting vote. Reg. 88 says just the chairman, but the model article says *'chairman or other director chairing the meeting'*. The model article says that this does not apply if the chairman is not to be counted as participating in the decision-making process for quorum or voting purposes. This covers a situation where a director cannot participate (because of a conflict of interest for example) but acts as umpire and scorekeeper for the other directors. This exclusion is not mentioned in Reg. 88 of Table A.

The first draft of the model articles proposed discontinuing the chairman's casting vote, but this was later changed and it was not removed.

Article 14 – Conflicts of interest

This has many similarities with Regs. 94 to 98 of Table A, though there are some differences. This is more restrictive and does not allow a director who has declared an interest in a transaction or arrangement with the company to participate for quorum or voting purposes when the particular item of business is before the directors' meeting. Some companies may wish to vary this article.

Article 15 – Records of decisions to be kept

This repeats the provisions of CA2006 section 248 that minutes must be taken and kept for at least 10 years. It corresponds with Reg. 100 of Table A, but Reg. 100 mentions meetings rather than decisions. Reg. 100 mentions a few detailed requirements, whereas the model articles mention unanimous or majority decisions. Perhaps surprisingly, the model article does not mention the need to record the names of directors present or participating.

Article 16 – Directors' discretion to make further rules

This is an admirably succinct provision and it is also extremely important. In different words it corresponds with part of Reg. 88 of Table A.

Appointment of directors (Articles 17-20)

Article 17 – Methods of appointing directors

This is like Regs. 78 and 79 of Table A in that the members appoint directors by ordinary resolution and the directors themselves may appoint directors. Table A states that directors may only appoint up to any maximum number of directors fixed by the articles. It is obviously unnecessary to say this and it is sensibly not included in this article.

Reg. 76 of Table A provides that, unless a proposed director is recommended by the directors, notice of certain particulars must within a certain time period be given to the members. This requirement is omitted from the model articles.

There is new provision (with no corresponding provision in Table A) for dealing with the situation where the company has no shareholders and no directors. This will only be needed in a very small number of cases, but it could be very important and is to be welcomed.

Article 18 – Termination of director's appointment

This repeats some of the provisions of CA2006 in the same way that the corresponding article in Table A (Reg. 81) repeats some of the provisions of CA1985. This seems unnecessary but is presumably for educational purposes. The new article differs from Table A in the following respects:

- Reference is made to a registered medical practitioner giving a written opinion that a director has become physically or mentally incapable of acting as a director, and may remain so for more than three months. There is no mention of physical health in Reg. 81.
- Provision for the position when a director has a mental disorder is different.
- Table A allows the directors to remove a director if he has been absent from meetings of directors for more than six consecutive months. This provision is not included in the model articles.

The Table A provision concerning a director missing board meetings for six months was much criticised and many people were glad to see it go. It meant that in a company having weekly board meetings a director could not be removed on these grounds if he missed 25 out of 26. On the other hand, in a company having two board meetings a year a director whose train was cancelled would be vulnerable.

Article 18's treatment of physical and mental health issues seems more sensible than the treatment in Table A. It is interesting to note that statutory law does not cause a person detained under the Mental Health Act to cease being a director. This only happens if it is a provision of the articles. CA2006 does not require that a person who makes a composition with his creditors generally (an IVA for example) ceases to be a director. It only happens if it is in the articles. There is nothing in the model articles to stop a person coming off the board being put straight back on. I am aware of a director who signed an IVA at 10.00 am, came off the board as required by the articles and was put back on at 2.00 pm on the same day.

Article 19 – Directors' remuneration

The corresponding regulations in Table A are Regs. 82, 84 and 87, particularly Reg. 82. This states that directors shall be entitled to such remuneration as the company may by ordinary resolution determine. In practice in many companies this requirement is circumnavigated or even ignored. There is no mention of this in Article 19 which allows directors' remuneration to be fixed by the directors themselves.

Article 20 – Directors' expenses

This is essentially the same as Reg. 83 of Table A, though this article uses the words 'reasonable' and 'properly incur'. In *'Young v Naval, Military and Civil Service Co-operative Society of South Africa 1905'* it was held that directors only have the right to be reimbursed for expenses if there is provision for it in the articles.

Shares (Articles 21-29)

Article 21 – All shares to be fully paid up

These articles, unlike Table A, do not provide for the possibility of partly paid shares. However, rather surprisingly partly paid or nil paid shares may be taken on the formation of the company by the subscribers to the memorandum. Again rather surprisingly, there is no mention of how such shares may later be paid up.

Article 22 – Powers to issue different classes of share

This differs from Regs. 2 and 3 in Table A. In particular, if redeemable shares are issued, the directors may determine the terms, conditions and manner of redemption.

The case of *'Bushell v Faith 1970'* illustrates that it is possible to issue shares with rights that vary in certain circumstances. A company had three shareholders, Mr Bushell and his two sisters having 100 shares each. The articles specified that on a resolution to remove Mr Bushell as a director, each of his shares carried three votes. His sisters did wish to remove him as a director and on a show of hands the resolution was passed by two votes to one. Mr Bushell called for a poll and maintained that the resolution was defeated by 300 votes to 200. The House of Lords upheld Mr Bushell's contention and accepted the validity of the article.

Article 23 – Company not bound by less than absolute interests

This is self-explanatory and in slightly different words has the same effect as Reg. 5 of Table A.

Article 24 – Share certificates

This article corresponds with Reg. 6 of Table A but it requires that the certificate state that the shares are fully paid. Table A allows for the possibility of the shares being partly paid. Also, it requires the certificate to state the nominal value of the shares and allows certificates to be *'otherwise executed in accordance with the Companies Acts'*.

Article 25 – Replacement share certificates

This corresponds with Reg. 7 of Table A but there are the following differences:

- A shareholder may at the same time exercise the right to be issued with a single certificate or separate certificates. Reg. 7 does not mention this.
- The company may make a reasonable charge. Reg. 7 does not allow this. It is interesting to note that the 1948 Table A permits a charge not to exceed two shillings and six pence.

A shareholder requiring a replacement share certificate must comply with such conditions and evidence as the directors decide.

Article 26 – Share transfers

This is a very important article and there is a very significant departure from Table A. The corresponding regulations in Table A are Regs. 23 to 28.

This article gives directors the right to refuse to transfer a share and there is no requirement that they give a reason. Table A only gives the directors this right if the shares are partly paid or if the company has a lien on them.

Both Article 26 and Table A require a refused instrument of transfer to be returned to the transferee. However, unlike Table A Article 26 allows the directors to retain it if they suspect that the proposed transfer may be fraudulent.

Table A states that notice of a refused transfer must be sent within two months. This is not in Article 26 because it is a requirement of CA2006.

Table A states that transfers may be suspended for up to 30 days in any year. That is not mentioned in this article.

If directors are considering refusing to accept a share transfer, they should keep in mind their general duties. Section 172 of CA2006 requires them to promote the success of the company for the benefit of the members as a whole. If they do refuse a transfer, it should be because they believe it to be in the company's interest, not because of their self-interest or because of a private quarrel.

Articles 27-29 – Transmission of shares and associated provisions

These articles correspond with Regs. 29 to 31 of Table A. They are essentially the same but Table A does not make it clear that transmittees are bound by prior notices.

Dividends and other distributions (Articles 30-35)

These articles correspond with Regs. 102 to 108 in Table A and have substantially the same effect, though unlike Table A there is no mention of partly paid shares. Directors may pay interim dividends, but final dividends have to be approved by an ordinary resolution of the shareholders and cannot be more than the directors recommend. This restriction is in any case thought to be the case law position. Of course in most private companies final dividends are in practice rare and shareholders are rewarded exclusively by interim dividends. Any number of interim dividends may be paid.

Reg. 106 of Table A deals exclusively with the payment of dividends by cheque, whereas Article 31 also deals with payment by bank transfer or other means. In view of the banks' controversial and much criticised ambitions to phase out the use of cheques this is just as well.

Article 30(4) states that unless the shareholders' or directors' resolution or the terms of issue of the shares specify otherwise, a dividend must be paid according to shareholdings registered at the date that the dividend resolution is passed. This is not in Table A and it is helpful and important. There may be scope for disputes if shares are sold before the declaration of a dividend and the register of members has not been changed. This is one reason why dividend resolutions should be tightly drafted.

Capitalisation of profits (Article 36)

This is essentially the same as Reg. 110 of Table A, though Table A recognises the possibility of partly paid shares.

Organisation of general meetings (Articles 37-41)

Article 37 – Attendance and speaking at general meetings

This is both significant and new. Persons are able, subject to conditions, to participate in, speak at and vote at general meetings without being physically in each other's presence. Article 37(3) states '*In determining attendance at a general meeting, it is immaterial whether any two or more members attending it are in the same place as each other.*' This permits, among other things, telephone conference calls and real time e-mail meetings. It is suggested that real time communication is essential. A telephone meeting, for example, with a chairman relaying messages would probably not be permitted.

Article 38 – Quorum for general meetings

This corresponds with Reg. 40 of Table A in that business may not be transacted unless a quorum is present, though unlike Table A the appointment of a chairman is an exception.

CA2006 section 318 states that in a sole-member limited company the presence of one qualifying member at a meeting will constitute a quorum. This will take precedence over any higher number specified by the articles. Section 318 also states that in any other case two qualifying persons present at a meeting will constitute a quorum, but this may be varied by any other number specified by the articles. Article 38 does not specify a number, so a quorum will be two or one if it is a sole-member company.

Article 39 – Chairing a general meeting

This corresponds with Regs. 42 and 43 of Table A. The chairman does not have an inherent right to a casting vote and only has one if it is conferred by the articles, which this article does not do. Table A for companies incorporated prior to 1st October 2007 does give the chairman a casting vote, but Table A for companies incorporated from that date (which is the version reproduced in Appendix C) does not. Some authorities believe that the legal position is that in a company incorporated on or after 1st October 2007 the chairman may only have a casting vote if he is a member.

Article 40 – Attendance and speaking by directors and non-shareholders

This corresponds with Reg. 44 of Table A in that directors may attend and speak at general meetings, whether or not they are shareholders. Many would argue that, if permitted, directors have a duty to do this in order to account for their actions.

This article goes further and allows, which Table A does not specifically do, the chairman to extend this to persons who are not directors. This can be very useful in, for example, allowing a legal adviser to advise a meeting.

Article 41 – Adjournment

This corresponds with Regs. 41 and 45 of Table A, but there are some important differences.

- The chairman may adjourn if it appears to him that an adjournment is necessary to protect the safety of any person attending the meeting or ensure that the business of the meeting is conducted in an orderly manner. This has been regarded as an inherent common law right, but it is not in Table A.
- Article 41 specifies in detail to whom notice of an adjourned meeting must be given. Table A does not do this.

Voting at general meetings (Articles 42-47)

Article 42 – Voting general

It is becoming increasingly common for articles to stipulate that votes on most resolutions go straight to a poll, bypassing the show of hands. However, this article (like Reg. 46 in Table A) requires a show of hands. This of course does not prevent the vote subsequently going to a poll if there is a valid demand.

Article 43 – Errors and disputes

This is the same as Reg. 58 in Table A.

Article 44 – Poll votes

Polls are covered in Regs. 45 to 52 in Table A so this single article must count as a triumph of brevity. The rules are generally the same as in Table A, but Article 44 allows the directors to call for a poll and for a poll to be demanded in advance of the meeting. These provisions are not in Table A.

Reg. 46(d) of Table A allows a member or members holding shares conferring a right to vote at the meeting being shares on which an aggregate sum has been paid up equal to not less than one tenth of the total sum paid up on all the shares to call for a poll. This is not in Article 44, though a demand by a member or members representing not less than one tenth of the total voting rights of all the members having the right to vote at the meeting is in both Table A and Article 44.

Article 45 – Content of proxy notices

This has many similarities with Regs. 60-62 of Table A. However this article, unlike Table A, does not provide specimen forms. Table A provides two, for use according to whether or not the proxy is given instructions how to vote. These forms, though, are not compulsory and it is permitted to use *'a form as near thereto as circumstances allow or in any other form which is usual or which the directors may approve'*. Article 45 states that proxy instructions must be in writing and it lists some essential details, but then allows discretion.

Article 46 – Delivery of proxy notices

This is essentially the same as Table A.

Article 47 – Amendment to resolutions

This is a completely new article with no corresponding regulation in Table A. It has been generally welcomed.

Administrative arrangements (Articles 48-51)

Article 48 – Means of communication to be used

This article is much shorter than the corresponding Regs. 111 to 116 in Table A and it contains the following two provisions that are not in Table A:

- Any notice or document sent to or by a director may be sent in a manner requested by the director.
- Directors may agree with the company that notices or documents are deemed to be received within a specified time of their being sent.

There are a number of provisions in Table A not replicated in Reg. 48, but although the wording is different the key elements concerning communication with the members are the same.

Article 49 – Company seals

This corresponds with Reg. 101 of Table A but there are some significant differences as follows:

- Article 49 states '*The directors may decide by what means and in what form any common seal is to be used*'. This is close to, but not exactly the same as, Reg. 101.
- Article 49 states that unless otherwise decided by the directors, the document must be signed by at least one authorised person in the presence of a witness. 'Authorised person' is defined as any director, the company secretary (if any) and any person authorised for the purpose by the directors. Reg. 101 states, unless otherwise determined by the directors, any two directors or one director and the company secretary.

Article 50 – No right to inspect the accounts or other records

This has exactly the same effect as Reg. 109 of Table A. Other than as provided by law or with the authority of an ordinary resolution of the shareholders, only the directors and (if applicable) the auditor have the right to inspect the accounts or other records.

Article 51 – Provision for employees on cessation of business

This is not in Table A and it empowers directors to look after present or former employees, over and above any contractual commitments, in the circumstances specified.

Directors' indemnity and insurance (Articles 52-53)

Article 52 – Indemnity

Rather confusingly the section of the model articles is headed as shown above, but the content of Article 52 goes beyond just directors and relates to 'a relevant officer of the company or an associated company'. This is perhaps just as well for some company secretaries and other officers who are not directors. Reg. 118 is the corresponding regulation in Table A and this refers to 'every director or other officer or auditor'.

Article 52 extends the indemnity to a relevant officer of an associated company as defined. Reg. 118 does not do this.

Article 52(1b) makes it explicit that the indemnity is extended to activity as trustee of an occupational pension scheme. Reg. 118 does not do this.

The following words in the article should be particularly noted:

> *'This article does not authorise any indemnity which would be prohibited or rendered void by any provision of the Companies Acts or by any other provision of law'.*

CA2006 renders void an attempt by the company to indemnify a director from a successful civil action for negligence, default, breach of duty or trust. Section 232(1) of the Act reads:

> *'Any provision that purports to exempt a director of a company (to any extent) from any liability that would otherwise attach to him in connection with any negligence, default, breach of duty or breach of trust in relation to the company is void.'*

Article 53 – Insurance

CA2006 Section 233 permits a company to purchase and maintain insurance for a director, including insurance for an action by the company for negligence, default, breach of duty or trust. This can be done unless the articles prohibit it. Not only does Article 53 not prohibit it, it specifically allows it and extends it to relevant officers of associated companies.

Model articles for private companies limited by guarantee

These articles are virtually identical to the model articles for private companies limited by shares, though the numbers of the individual articles are different and there is no mention of shares or dividends. The following points are worthy of note:

Article 2 – Liability of members

There is no corresponding provision in Table C because until 1st October 2009 the statement of limited liability was contained in the memorandum. It is important that this is not omitted if the articles are changed.

The members can of course substitute any sum for the stated liability limit of £1. However, it is typical of many companies limited by guarantee. It is such a nominal sum that in the event of an insolvency, the cost of collection would undoubtedly exceed the amount collected. To put this into context 83 per cent of private companies limited by shares have an issued share capital of £100 or less.

Article 21 – Applications for membership

This is, in the main, the same as Reg. 3 of Table C, though it is expressed differently and is perhaps easier to follow. Table C says that the subscribers to the memorandum of association will be members and this is not repeated in this article.

Article 22 – Termination of membership

This has the same effect as Reg. 4 of Table C, but it uses the sinister-sounding phrase 'when that person ceases to exist'. It covers, for example, the liquidation of a company that is a member.

A Thorogood Special Briefing

Chapter 8
Review of model articles for public companies

- Introduction
- Liability of members (Article 2)
- Directors' powers and responsibilities (Articles 3-6)
- Decision-making by directors (Articles 7-19)
- Appointment of directors (Articles 20-24)
- Alternate directors (Articles 25-27)
- Organisation of general meetings (Articles 28-33)
- Voting at general meetings (Articles 34-40)
- Restrictions on members' rights (Article 41)
- Application of rules to class meetings (Article 42)
- Issue of shares (Articles 43-44)
- Interests in shares (Article 45)
- Share certificates (Articles 46-49)
- Shares not held in certificated form (Articles 50-51)
- Partly paid shares (Articles 52-62)
- Transfer and transmission of shares (Articles 63-68)
- Consolidation of shares (Article 69)
- Distributions (Articles 70-77)
- Capitalisation of profits (Article 78)
- Communications (Articles 79-80)
- Administrative arrangements (Articles 81-84)
- Directors' indemnity and insurance (Articles 85-86)

Chapter 8
Review of model articles for public companies

Introduction

Hardly any companies at all use the model articles for public companies without modification. There are a number of reasons for this. Firstly, and despite their importance, only 0.3 per cent of registered companies are public companies. It is a relatively small number and most of them were incorporated before 1st October 2009. This means that unless steps were taken to alter it, Table A is their default provision. Secondly, many public companies were formed as private companies and then re-registered. Unless steps are taken to change it the private company model articles will remain their default provision. A third reason is that the unamended model articles are not suitable for listed companies.

The model articles for public companies are mainly used as a template for people drafting or amending articles. They are a rich seam that may be mined for that purpose and, although it is an inexcusable mixed metaphor, they may be cherry-picked. As they are model articles sanctioned by Regulations the drafting may be relied upon to have the intended legal effect.

This chapter consists of a review of these model articles. If you have read the previous chapter, some of what follows will be familiar. This is because some of these model articles are the same as (or very close to) corresponding articles in the model articles for private companies limited by shares. I have not changed the review just for the sake of having different words.

Liability of members (Article 2)

This is the same as Article 2 in the model articles for private companies limited by shares. There is no corresponding provision in Table A because until 1st October 2009 the statement of limited liability was contained in the memorandum. It is important that this is not omitted if the articles are changed.

Directors' powers and responsibilities (Articles 3-6)

This section of the model articles gives directors the power to run the company. It is, in general, close to Table A but the power to delegate is more extensive and more explicit.

Article 3 – Directors' general authority

This article gives the directors full authority to manage the company's business, subject to the reserve power of the shareholders (Article 4). It is generally accepted that the directors need this authority and this article, but it is possible to limit the authority in various ways. It is subject to the articles but the model articles place no restriction. This article has the same effect as the more wordy Reg. 70 of Table A.

Article 4 – Members' reserve power

Members only have this reserve power if it is provided by the articles. Any use of it by the members must be lawful and cannot have backdated effect.

Article 5 – Directors may delegate

Some delegation is essential in all but very small companies. Without it the business of the company would not be possible. This article goes further than Regs. 71 and 72 of Table A. The power to delegate is very wide and includes the power to delegate to persons who are not directors. The person or committee to whom delegation has been made may be authorised to delegate further. Of course some things may not be delegated. Signing the balance sheet is an example.

Article 6 – Committees

This requires committees to follow the rules applying to directors as far as they are applicable, and permits directors to make further rules for them. It is effectively the same as part of Reg. 72 of Table A.

Decision-making by directors (Articles 7-19)

Article 7 – Directors to take decisions collectively

Decisions are taken at a meeting or in the form of a directors' written resolution. These are the subject of Articles 17 and 18. Unlike the model articles for private companies limited by shares there is no provision for eligible directors communicating that they share a common view. CA2006 requires public companies to have at least two directors and accordingly there is no provision for the position when there is a sole director.

Article 8 – Calling a directors' meeting

This article says that any director may call a directors' meeting and that the company secretary 'must' do so if any director so requests. Article 9 in the model articles for private companies limited by shares says that any director may 'authorise' the company secretary (if any) to do so. It is a subtle distinction. This article, unlike Table A, does not say that notice need not be given to a director who is not in the United Kingdom.

Notice need not be in writing, but must specify date, time and place, and if all the directors will be in the same place, how it is proposed that they will communicate with each other.

Article 9 – Participation in a directors' meeting

This article has received a lot of attention and goes beyond the provisions of Table A. Subject to conditions '*it is irrelevant where any director is or how they communicate with each other*'. This permits telephone board meetings, video conference board meetings and real-time e-mail communication. It is suggested that some form of simultaneous communication is essential and that the article does not cover a chairman relaying the substance of telephone calls or exchanges of e-mails over a period. It is possible that in due course case law will clarify the limits of what is permitted.

The article includes, which Table A does not, '*If all the directors participating in a meeting are not in the same place, they may decide that the meeting is to be treated as taking place wherever one of them is*'. This means that five directors could be in England and one sipping cocktails on the beach in an exotic tax haven, and a board meeting is being held in the tax haven. In some companies it is important to show that control is exercised in a particular jurisdiction, and this could have important tax implications. However, your writer, though not a tax expert, suspects that the tax authorities will not lightly accept this resulting in a reduction of tax payable. An unwelcome consequence (for some) could be that directors have fewer reasons for spending time in tax havens.

Article 10 – Quorum for directors' meetings

The directors themselves may fix the number for a quorum, but in the absence of a decision it is two. This has the same effect as Regs. 89 and 90 of Table A, but there is no mention of alternate directors.

Article 11 – Meetings where total number of directors less than quorum

This goes into more detail than Reg. 90 of Table A

Article 12 – Chairing directors' meetings

This corresponds with Reg. 91 of Table A. Like Reg. 91 the directors may (but not must) appoint a chairman and may remove him from the position. Unlike Reg. 91 there is mention of appointing deputy and assistant chairmen. This article, unlike Reg. 91, requires the directors to appoint someone to chair the meeting if a duly appointed chairman, deputy or assistant is not present.

Article 13 – Voting at directors' meetings: general rules

This generally corresponds with the Table A position and it is one director one vote. In line with CA2006 a director may not vote on a matter if he has a conflict of interest.

Article 14 – Chairman's casting vote at directors' meetings

As with Reg. 88 of Table A, the chairman has a casting vote. Reg. 88 of Table A says just the chairman, but the model article says *'chairman or other director chairing the meeting'*. The model article says that this does not apply if the chairman is not to be counted as participating in the decision-making process for quorum or voting purposes. This covers a situation where a director cannot participate (because of a conflict of interest for example) but acts as umpire and scorekeeper for the directors. This exclusion is not mentioned in Reg. 88 of Table A.

The first draft of the model articles proposed discontinuing the chairman's casting vote, but this was later changed and it was not removed.

Article 15 – Alternates voting at a directors' meeting

This is self-explanatory and corresponds with the Table A position.

Article 16 – Conflicts of interest

Although there are some differences, this largely corresponds with Regs. 94-98 of Table A. CA2006 only permits the directors of a public company to authorise a director's conflict of interest if the articles or a shareholders' resolution says that they can. This article does not do that.

Article 17 – Proposing directors' written resolutions and Article 18 – Adoption of directors' written resolutions

Reg. 93 of Table A permits directors to make unanimous decisions by means of a written resolution. These articles have the same effect but are significantly longer and are more detailed and prescriptive. These articles, unlike the model articles for private companies limited by shares, do not allow the directors to make a decision by communicating to each other by any means a unanimously held view.

Article 19 – Directors' discretion to make further rules

This is an extremely important article and will be a great comfort to directors. It is the same as Article 16 in the model articles for private companies limited by shares and effectively the same as part of Reg. 88 in Table A.

Appointment of directors (Articles 20-24)

In fact these articles are more wide-ranging than the appointment of directors, but it is a matter of presentation and makes no practical difference.

Article 20 – Methods of appointing directors

This is like Regs. 78 and 79 of Table A in that the members appoint directors by ordinary resolution and the directors themselves may appoint directors. Table A states that directors may only appoint up to any maximum number of directors fixed by the articles. It is obviously unnecessary to say this and it is sensibly not included in this article.

Reg. 76 of Table A provides that, unless a proposed director is recommended by the directors, notice of certain particulars must within a certain time period be given to the members. This requirement is omitted from the model articles.

This article, unlike Article 17 in the model articles for private companies limited by shares, makes no provision for the eventuality of the company having no directors and no shareholders. It is presumably considered to be such a remote possibility in a public company that provision for it is unnecessary.

Article 21 – Retirement of directors by rotation

This continues (for public companies only) the requirement that directors retire by rotation and may offer themselves for reappointment. However, the identification of the directors to retire differs from the position under Table A.

Article 22 – Termination of a director's appointment

This repeats some of the provisions of CA2006 in the same way that the corresponding article in Table A (Reg. 81) repeats some of the provisions of CA1985. This seems unnecessary but is presumably for educational purposes. However, is it really necessary to state that a person who is prohibited from being a director by law ceases to be a director? There cannot be many people who do not know that. The new article differs from Table A in the following respects:

- Reference is made to a registered medical practitioner giving a written opinion that a director has become physically or mentally incapable of acting as a director, and may remain so for more than three months. There is no mention of physical health in Reg. 81.
- Provision for the position when a director has a mental disorder is different.
- Table A allows the directors to remove a director if he has been absent from meetings of directors for more than six consecutive months. This provision is not included in the model articles.

The Table A provision concerning a director missing board meetings for six months was much criticised and many people were glad to see it go. It meant that in a company having weekly board meetings a director could not be removed on these grounds if he missed 25 out of 26. On the other hand, in a company having two board meetings a year a director whose train was cancelled would be vulnerable.

Article 18's treatment of physical and mental health issues seems more sensible than the treatment in Table A. It is interesting to note that statutory law does not cause a person detained under the Mental Health Act to cease being a director. This only happens if it is a provision of the articles. CA2006 does not require that a person who makes a composition with his creditors generally (an IVA for example) ceases to be a director. It only happens if it is in the articles. There is nothing in the model articles to stop a person coming off the board being put straight back on. I am aware of a director who signed an IVA at 10.00 am, came off the board as required by the articles and was put back on at 2.00 pm on the same day.

Article 23 – Directors' remuneration

The corresponding regulations in Table A are Regs. 82, 84 and 87, particularly Reg. 82. This states that directors shall be entitled to such remuneration as the company may by ordinary resolution determine. There is no mention of this in this article which allows directors' remuneration to be fixed by the directors themselves.

Article 24 – Directors' expenses

This is essentially the same as Reg. 83 of Table A, though this article uses the words 'reasonable' and 'properly incur'. In *'Young v Naval, Military and Civil Service Co-operative Society of South Africa 1905'* it was held that directors only have the right to be reimbursed for expenses if there is provision for it in the articles.

Alternate directors (Articles 25-27)

These articles correspond with Regs. 65-69 of Table A, and although there are some subtle differences they say essentially the same. The model articles for private companies do not allow for alternate directors, and private companies wishing to permit them will probably incorporate these articles into their articles.

Organisation of general meetings (Articles 28-33)

Article 28 – Members can call general meeting if not enough directors

This deals with a situation where the number of directors has dropped below the statutory minimum and the remaining director (if any) is unable or unwilling to initiate steps to remedy the situation. It should be noted that the company secretary has no independent authority to convene a general meeting. This article has certain similarities with part of Reg. 37 of Table A but Table A allows a single member to call a general meeting in these circumstances. This article says two.

Article 29 – Attendance and speaking at general meetings

This is both significant and new. Persons are able, subject to conditions, to participate in, speak at and vote at general meetings without being physically in each other's presence. Article 29(4) states '*In determining attendance at a general meeting, it is immaterial whether any two or more members attending it are in the same place as each other*'. This permits, among other things, telephone conference calls and real time e-mail meetings. It is suggested that real time communication is essential. A telephone meeting, for example, with a chairman relaying messages would probably not be permitted.

Article 30 – Quorum for general meetings

This corresponds with Reg. 40 of Table A in that business may not be transacted unless a quorum is present, though unlike Table A the appointment of a chairman is an exception.

CA2006 section 318 states that in a sole-member limited company the presence of one qualifying member at a meeting will constitute a quorum. This will take precedence over any higher number specified by the articles. Section 318 also states that in any other case two qualifying persons present at a meeting will constitute a quorum, but this may be varied by any other number specified by the articles. Article 38 does not specify a number, so a quorum will be two or one if it is a sole-member company.

Article 31 – Chairing general meetings

This corresponds with Regs. 42 and 43 of Table A. The chairman does not have an inherent right to a casting vote and only has one if it is conferred by the articles, which this article does not do. Table A for companies incorporated prior to 1st October 2007 does give the chairman a casting vote, but Table A for companies incorporated from that date (which is the version reproduced in Appendix C) does not. Some authorities believe that the legal position is that in a company incorporated on or after 1st October 2007 the chairman may only have a casting vote if he is a member.

Article 32 – Attendance and speaking by directors and non-members

This corresponds with Reg. 44 of Table A in that directors may attend and speak at general meetings, whether or not they are shareholders. Many would argue that, if permitted, directors have a duty to do this in order to account for their actions.

This article goes further and allows, which Table A does not specifically do, the chairman to extend this to persons who are not directors. This can be very useful in, for example, allowing a legal adviser to advise a meeting.

Article 33 – Adjournment

This corresponds with Regs. 41 and 45 of Table A, but there are some important differences:

- The chairman may adjourn if it appears to him that an adjournment is necessary to protect the safety of any person attending the meeting or ensure that the business of the meeting is conducted in an orderly manner. This has been regarded as an inherent common law right, but it is not in Table A.
- Article 41 specifies in detail to whom notice of an adjourned meeting must be given. Table A does not do this.

Voting at general meetings (Articles 34-40)

Article 34 – Voting: general

Voting is initially on a show of hands with each voting person present having one vote, regardless of the number of shares that he owns or represents. The chairman should announce the result and if there is not a valid demand for a poll, this will be the decision made. It is becoming increasingly common for the articles of companies, especially public companies, to bypass a show of hands and move straight to a poll.

Article 35 – Errors and disputes

This is the same as Reg. 58 in Table A.

Article 36 – Demanding a poll

This is self-explanatory. It should be noted that this article, unlike Table A, allows the directors (acting collectively) to demand a poll.

Article 37 – Procedure on a poll

This too is self-explanatory.

Article 38 – Content of proxy notices

This has many similarities with Regs. 60-62 of Table A. However, this article, unlike Table A, does not provide specimen forms. Table A provides two, for use according to whether or not the proxy is given instructions how to vote. These forms, though, are not compulsory and it is permitted to use *'a form as near thereto as circumstances allow or in any other form which is usual or which the directors may approve'*. This article states that proxy instructions must be in writing and it lists some essential details, but then allows discretion.

Article 39 – Delivery of proxy notices

This goes into considerable detail – more detail than the model articles for private companies limited by shares.

Article 40 – Amendments to resolutions

This is a new article with no corresponding regulation in Table A. It is considered useful and has been generally welcomed.

Restrictions on members' rights (Article 41)

Article 41 – No voting on shares on which money owed to the company

This is self-explanatory.

Application of rules to class meetings (Article 42)

Article 42 – Class meetings

This does exactly what it says in a single sentence, and extends the rules to any meetings of holders of a particular class of shares.

Issue of shares (Articles 43-44)

Article 43 – Powers to issue different classes of shares

This differs from Regs. 2 and 3 in Table A. In particular, if redeemable shares are issued, the directors may determine the terms, conditions and manner of redemption.

The case of '*Bushell v Faith 1970*' illustrates that it is possible to issue shares with rights that vary in certain circumstances. A company had three shareholders, Mr Bushell and his two sisters having 100 shares each. The articles specified that on a resolution to remove Mr Bushell as a director, each of his shares carried three votes. His sisters did wish to remove him as a director and on a show of hands the resolution was passed by two votes to one. Mr Bushell called for a poll and maintained that the resolution was defeated by 300 votes to 200. The House of Lords upheld Mr Bushell's contention and accepted the validity of the article.

Article 44 – Payment of commissions on subscription for shares

This is self-explanatory and is essentially the same as Reg. 4 of Table A.

Interests in shares (Article 45)

Article 45 – Company not bound by less than absolute interests

This is self-explanatory and in slightly different words has the same effect as Reg. 5 of Table A.

Share certificates (Articles 46-49)

Article 46 – Certificates to be issued except in certain cases

This corresponds with part of Reg. 6 of Table A but it is more up to date and better laid out. Unlike Table A it lists the types of shares to which it does not relate.

Article 47 – Contents and execution of share certificates

This also corresponds with part of Reg. 6 of Table A and it too is better laid out. Unlike Reg. 6, it mentions the possibility of execution without the company seal.

Article 48 – Consolidated share certificates

This, helpfully and at considerable length, deals with the possibilities, rights and obligations when a member has more than one holding of a class of share. There is a minor reference in Reg. 6 of Table A.

Article 49 – Replacement share certificates

This corresponds with Reg. 7 of Table A but there are the following differences:

- A shareholder may at the same time exercise the right to be issued with a single certificate or separate certificates. Reg. 7 does not mention this.
- The company may make a reasonable charge. Reg. 7 does not allow this. It is interesting to note that the 1948 Table A permits a charge not to exceed two shillings and six pence.

A shareholder requiring a replacement share certificate must comply with such conditions and evidence as the directors decide.

Shares not held in certificated form (Articles 50-51)

Article 50 – Uncertificated shares and Article 51 – Share warrants

These articles set out the rules for uncertificated shares in some detail. There are no corresponding provisions in Table A.

Partly paid shares (Articles 52-62)

There is no provision for partly paid shares in the model articles for private companies limited by shares.

Article 52 – Company's lien over partly paid shares

This is essentially the same as Reg. 8 of Table A. companies sometimes amend this article to give a lien over all shares – not just partly paid shares.

Article 53 – Enforcement of the company's lien

This corresponds with Regs. 9-11 of Table A. The new model article seems clearer and better drafted.

Article 54 – Call notices, Article 55 – Liability to pay calls and Article 56 – When call notice need not be issued

These articles broadly correspond with Regs. 12-17 of Table A, though they seem better laid out and there are some differences. The following points might well be noted:

- A member may not be required to pay more than the total sum unpaid on his shares.
- A member may not be required to pay the call before 14 days from the date that the call notice was sent.
- Liability to pay a call is not extinguished by transferring the shares.

Articles 57 – 62 – Relating to failure to comply with calls, forfeiture and surrender of shares

These articles correspond with Regs. 18-22 of Table A. They are longer and set out the relevant points clearly. As with Table A, interest is payable if a call is paid late.

Transfer and transmission of shares (Articles 63-68)

Transfer involves the sale of shares to a willing buyer or the gift of shares to a willing recipient. Transmission involves a change in the registered owner due to the process of law (death, bankruptcy etc).

Article 63 – Transfer of certificated shares

This corresponds with Regs. 23 to 28 of Table A. Like Table A (but unlike the model articles for private companies) directors do not have discretion to refuse a transfer, unless the shares are partly paid.

A new provision is that although the directors must normally return the instrument of transfer to the transferee if the transfer is refused, they need not do so if they suspect that the proposed transfer may be fraudulent.

Article 64 – Transfer of uncertificated shares

Directors may refuse to transfer a share if it is in favour of more than four transferees. They must do so if such a transfer is of uncertificated shares.

Articles 65-67 – Transmission of shares

These model articles correspond with Regs. 29-31 of Table A. There are a few minor differences but they are substantially the same.

Article 68 – Transmittees bound by prior notices

There is no equivalent provision in Table A.

Consolidation of shares (Article 69)

Article 69 – Procedure for disposing of fractions of shares

This corresponds with Reg. 33 of Table A but there is nothing in Reg. 33 about authorising a member's portion to be distributed to charity.

Distributions (Articles 70-77)

Article 70 – Procedure for declaring dividends

This corresponds with Regs. 102 and 103 of Table A. It confirms what is thought to be the common law position that shareholders cannot have dividends greater than the amount recommended by the directors, which has to be sensible. It could be dangerous to let some shareholders loose in the sweetshop. They might take too many sweets. Directors may declare and pay any number of interim dividends but the final dividend (if any) must be recommended by the directors and approved by the members.

Subsection (4) helpfully specifies that unless the members' resolution or directors' decision specifies otherwise a dividend must be paid according to the register of members at the time that the resolution is passed or the decision made. This is to settle disputes that may arise if shares have been sold but the transfer has not yet been registered.

Article 71 – Calculation of dividends

This corresponds with Reg. 104 of Table A, except that the reference to amounts paid up in advance is new.

Article 72 – Payment of dividends and other distributions

This is the same as Article 31 in the model articles for private companies limited by shares and it corresponds with Reg. 106 in Table A. However, Reg. 106 deals exclusively with the payment of dividends by cheque, whereas this article also deals with payment by bank transfer or other means. In view of the banks' controversial and much criticised ambitions to phase out the use of cheques this is just as well.

Article 73 – Deductions from distributions in respect of sums owed to the company

There is no corresponding article in Table A.

Article 74 – No interest on distributions

This is effectively the same as Reg. 107 of Table A.

Article 75 – Unclaimed distributions

This is based on Reg. 108 of Table A. However, Reg. 108 says that the directors may decide that if a dividend has been unclaimed for 12 years, it shall be forfeited. Article 75 says that it ceases to remain owing by the company and there is no mention of directors' discretion. The first part of Article 75 allows the directors to invest or otherwise make use of dividends that have not been claimed. This is not in Table A.

Article 76 – Non-cash distributions

The core of this model article is the same as Reg. 105 of Table A. However this model article contains additional provisions. Non-cash distributions could, for example, encompass a pro-rata distribution of the company's stock. So, for example, a company that imports and sells champagne could distribute champagne to its shareholders rather than a cash dividend. What a lovely idea!

It was held in *'Wood v Odessa Waterworks Co 1889'* that a dividend has to be paid in cash unless the articles say differently. Article 76 does say differently. Article 76 only allows a non-cash distribution to be made on the recommendation of the directors, and with the authority of an ordinary resolution.

Article 77 – Waiver of distributions

There is no corresponding provision in Table A.

Capitalisation of profits (Article 78)

This is the same as Article 36 in the model articles for private companies limited by shares, except that the public company model article allows for paying up existing shares. It is essentially the same as Reg. 110 of Table A.

Communications (Articles 79-80)

Article 79 – Means of communication to be used

This article is much shorter than the corresponding Regs. 111 to 116 in Table A and it contains the following two provisions that are not in Table A:

- Any notice or document sent to or by a director may be sent in a manner requested by the director.
- Directors may agree with the company that notices or documents are deemed to be received within a specified time of their being sent.

There are a number of provisions in Table A not replicated in Reg. 48, but although the wording is different the key elements concerning communication with the members are the same.

Article 80 – Failure to notify contact details

This is not in Table A and it is potentially very useful. It is high on the list of provisions that might well be considered for inclusion in the articles of private companies. Loss of contact with some members can be an issue in many companies.

Administrative arrangements (Articles 81-84)

Article 81 – Company seals

This article is much fuller than the corresponding regulation in Table A (Reg. 101). It states *'The directors may decide by what means and in what form any common seal is to be used'*. This is close to, but not exactly the same as, Reg. 101. It also states that unless otherwise decided by the directors, the document must be signed by at least one authorised person in the presence of a witness. 'Authorised person' is defined as any director, the company secretary (if any) and any person authorised for the purpose by the directors. Reg. 101 states, unless otherwise determined by the director, any two directors or one director and the company secretary.

Article 82 – Destruction of documents

This detailed and potentially helpful article is new.

Article 83 – No right to inspect accounts and other records

This has exactly the same effect as Reg. 109 of Table A. Other than as provided by law or with the authority of an ordinary resolution of the shareholders, only the directors and the auditor have the right to inspect the accounts or other records.

Article 84 – Provision for employees on cessation of business

This is not in Table A and it empowers directors to look after present or former employees, over and above any contractual commitments, in the circumstances specified.

Directors' indemnity and insurance (Articles 85-86)

Article 85 – Indemnity

This corresponds with Reg. 118 of Table A, but it extends the indemnity to a relevant director of an associated company. It also makes it explicit that the indemnity is extended to activity as trustee of an occupational pension scheme. Reg. 118 does not do that.

The following words in the article should be particularly noted

> *'This article does not authorise any indemnity which would be prohibited or rendered void by any provision of the Companies Acts or by any other provision of law'.*

CA2006 renders void an attempt by the company to indemnify a director from a successful civil action for negligence, default, breach of duty or trust. Section 232(1) of the Act reads

> *'Any provision that purports to exempt a director of a company (to any extent) from any liability that would otherwise attach to him in connection with any negligence, default, breach of duty or breach of trust in relation to the company is void.'*

Article 53 – Insurance

CA2006 Section 233 permits a company to purchase and maintain insurance for a director, including insurance for an action by the company for negligence, default, breach of duty or trust. This can be done unless the articles prohibit it. Not only does Article 53 not prohibit it, it specifically allows it and extends it to relevant officers of associated companies.

A Thorogood Special Briefing

Appendices

APPENDIX A
Cross-referencing of model articles for private companies limited by shares with the 1985 table A

MODEL ARTICLES FOR PRIVATE COMPANIES LIMITED BY SHARES	1985 TABLE A
1. Defined terms	1. Interpretation
2. Liability of members	N/A
3. Directors' general authority 4. Shareholders' reserve power	70. Powers of directors
5. Directors may delegate 6. Committees	71. Power to appoint agents 72. Delegation of directors' powers
7. Directors to take decisions collectively 8. Unanimous decisions 9. Calling a directors' meeting 10. Participation in directors' meetings 11. Quorum for directors' meetings	88. Proceedings of directors 93. Written resolution of directors 88. Proceedings of directors 89. Quorum for directors' meetings 90. Continuing directors may act to fill vacancies or call a general meeting
12. Chairing of directors' meetings	91. Chairing of directors' meetings
13. Casting vote	88. Proceedings of directors
14. Conflicts of interest	94-98. Conflicts of interest
15. Records of decisions to be kept	100. Minutes
16. Directors' discretion to make further rules	88. Proceedings of directors
17. Methods of appointing directors	76-80. Appointment and retirement of directors
18. Termination of director's appointment	81. Disqualification and removal of directors
19. Directors' remuneration	82. Remuneration of directors 84. Directors' appointments 87. Directors' gratuities and pensions
20. Directors' expenses	83. Directors' expenses
21. All shares to be fully paid up	N/A
22. Powers to issue different classes of share	2-3. Share capital
23. Company not bound by less than absolute interests	5. Company not bound by less than absolute interests
24. Share certificates	6. Share certificates
25. Replacement share certificates	7. Replacement share certificates
26. Share transfers	23-28. Share transfers

MODEL ARTICLES FOR PRIVATE COMPANIES LIMITED BY SHARES	1985 TABLE A
27-29. Transmission of shares	29-31. Transmission of shares
30-35. Dividends and other distributions	102-108. Dividends
36. Capitalisation of profits	110. Capitalisation of profits
37. Attendance and speaking at general meetings 38. Quorum for general meetings	40. Quorum at general meetings
39. Chairing general meetings	42-43. Chairing general meetings
40. Attendance and speaking by directors and non-shareholders	44. Attendance and speaking by directors
41. Adjournment	41 & 45. Adjournment
42. Voting: general 43. Errors and disputes	46. Voting: general 58. Objection to qualification of any voter
44. Poll votes	46-52. Polls
45. Content of proxy notices 46. Delivery of proxy notices	60-62. Appointment of proxies 63. Determination of proxy
47. Amendments to resolutions	N/A
48. Means of communication to be used	111-116. Notices
49. Company seals	101. The seal
50. No right to inspect accounts	109. No right to inspect accounts
51. Provision for employees on cessation	N/A
52. Indemnity 53. Insurance	118. Indemnity

APPENDIX B
Cross-referencing of 1985 table A with model articles for private companies limited by shares

1985 TABLE A	MODEL ARTICLES FOR PRIVATE COMPANIES LIMITED BY SHARES
1. Interpretation	1. Defined terms
	2. Liability of members
2-3. Share capital	22. Powers to issue different classes of share
4. Power to pay commissions	N/A – see ss. 552 & 553
5. Company not bound by less than absolute interests	23. Company not bound by less than absolute interests
6. Share certificates	24. Share certificates
7. Replacement share certificates	25. Replacement share certificates
8-11. Lien 12-17. Calls on shares 18-22. Forfeiture	N/A
23-28. Share transfers	26. Share transfers
29-31. Transmission of shares	27. Transmission of shares 28. Exercise of transmittees' rights 29. Transmittees bound by prior notices
32-33. Alteration of share capital	N/A – see ss. 617 & 618
34. Power to reduce capital	N/A – see s. 641
35. Power to purchase own shares	N/A – see s. 690
36. Extraordinary general meetings	N/A
37. Calling general meetings	N/A – see ss. 302-304
38. Notice of general meetings	N/A – see s. 307 (notice required), s. 311 (contents of notices of meetings) and s. 310 (persons entitled to receive notice of meetings)
39. Notice – accidental omission	N/A – see s. 313
40. Quorum – general meetings	37. Attendance and speaking at general meetings 38. Quorum for general meetings See also s. 318
41. Adjournment if no quorum present	41. Adjournment
42-43. Chairing general meetings	39. Chairing general meetings
44. Attendance and speaking by directors	40. Attendance and speaking by directors and non-shareholders

1985 TABLE A	MODEL ARTICLES FOR PRIVATE COMPANIES LIMITED BY SHARES
45. Adjournment	41. Adjournment
46. Voting: general 46. Demand for a poll 47. Declaration by the chairman of result on a show of hands 48. Demand for poll may be withdrawn 49. Method of taking poll	42. Voting: general 44. Poll votes See also s. 320 (declaration by chairman on a show of hands), 321 (right to demand a poll), 322 (voting on a poll) and 329 (right of proxy to demand a poll)
50. Chairman's casting vote	N/A
51. Timing of certain polls 52. Notice of a poll	44(4). Poll votes
53. Members' written resolutions	N/A – see ss. 288-300
54. Votes of members	N/A – see ss. 284-287
55. Votes of joint holders	N/A – see s. 286
56. Voting by member subject to a mental health order	See Article 27(3)
57. No votes on shares unless all moneys presently payable have been paid	N/A – all shares must be fully paid
58. Objection to qualification of any voter	43. Errors and disputes
59. Voting by proxies on a poll	N/A – see ss. 284-287 & 322
60-62. Appointment of proxies 63. Determination of proxy	45. Content of proxy notices 46. Delivery of proxy notices
	47. Amendments to resolutions
64. Number of directors	N/A
65-69. Alternate directors	N/A
70. Powers of directors	3. Directors' general authority 4. Shareholders' reserve power
71. Power to appoint agents 72. Delegation of directors' powers	5. Directors may delegate 6. Committees
76-78. Appointment by members 79. Appointment by directors	17. Methods of appointing directors
80. Retiring director continues in office until end of meeting	N/A
81. Disqualification and removal of directors	18. Termination of directors' appointment
82. Remuneration of directors	19. Directors' remuneration
83. Directors' expenses	20. Directors' expenses
84. Directors' appointments	19. Directors' remuneration
85-86. Directors' interests	N/A – see ss. 182-187

1985 TABLE A	MODEL ARTICLES FOR PRIVATE COMPANIES LIMITED BY SHARES
87. Directors' gratuities and pensions	See Article 19 above
88. Proceedings of directors	7. Directors to take decisions collectively 16. Directors' discretion to make further rules 9. Calling a directors' meeting
89. Quorum for directors' meetings 90. Continuing directors may act to fill vacancies or call a general meeting	10. Participation in directors meetings 11. Quorum for directors' meetings
91. Chairing of directors' meetings	12. Chairing of directors' meetings
92. Directors' acts valid, notwithstanding any defects	N/A – see s. 161
93. Written resolution of directors	8. Unanimous decisions
94. Conflicts of interest – voting 95. Director not counted in the quorum if not entitled to vote 96. Company may suspend or relax rules prohibiting a director from voting	14. Conflicts of interest
97. Appointment of two or more directors to offices or employments with the company	N/A
98. Questions as to the right of a director to vote to be referred to the chairman of the meeting	14(7). Conflicts of interest
99. Secretary	N/A
100. Minutes	See also s. 248 & ss. 355-359
101. The seal	49. Company seals
102. Declaration of dividends 103. Interim dividends 104. Apportionment of dividends 105. Non-cash distributions 106. Payment of dividends 107. No interest on distributions 108. Unclaimed distributions	30. Procedure for declaring dividends 31. Payment of dividends and other distributions 32. No interest on distributions 33. Unclaimed distributions 34. Non-cash distributions 35. Waiver of distributions
109. No right to inspect accounts and other records	50. No right to inspect accounts and other records
110. Capitalisation of profits	36. Capitalisation of profits
111-116. Notices	48. Means of communication to be used 29. Transmittees bound by prior notices
117. Winding-up – distribution of assets	N/A
	51. Provision for employees on cessation of business
118. Indemnity	52. Indemnity 53. Insurance

APPENDIX C
Table A to the Companies Act 1985 As amended by SI 2007/2541 and SI 2007/2826

REGULATIONS FOR MANAGEMENT OF A COMPANY LIMITED BY SHARES

VERSION FOR PRIVATE COMPANIES IN FORCE FROM 1ST OCTOBER 2007 TO 30TH SEPTEMBER 2009

1. In these regulations:
   - "the Act" means the Companies Act 1985 including any statutory modification or re-enactment thereof for the time being in force and any provisions of the Companies Act 2006 for the time being in force;
   - "the articles" means the articles of the company;
   - "clear days" in relation to the period of a notice means that period excluding the day when the notice is given or deemed to be given and the day for which it is given or on which it is to take effect;
   - "communication" means the same as in the Electronic Communications Act 2000;
   - "electronic communication" means the same as in the Electronic Communications Act 2000;
   - "executed" includes any mode of execution;
   - "office" means the registered office of the company;
   - "the holder" in relation to shares means the member whose name is entered in the register of members as the holder of the shares;
   - "the seal" means the common seal of the company;
   - "secretary" means the secretary of the company or any other person appointed to perform the duties of the secretary of the company, including a joint, assistant or deputy secretary;
   - "the United Kingdom" means Great Britain and Northern Ireland.

Unless the context otherwise requires, words or expressions contained in these regulations bear the same meaning as in the Act but excluding any statutory modification thereof not in force when these regulations become binding on the company.

SHARE CAPITAL

2. Subject to the provisions of the Act and without prejudice to any rights attached to any existing shares, any share may be issued with such rights or restrictions as the company may by ordinary resolution determine.

3. Subject to the provisions of the Act, shares may be issued which are to be redeemed or are to be liable to be redeemed at the option of the company or the holder on such terms and in such manner as may be provided by the articles.

4. The company may exercise the powers of paying commissions conferred by the Act. Subject to the provisions of the Act, any such commission may be satisfied by the payment of cash or by the allotment of fully or partly paid shares or partly in one way and partly in the other.

5. Except as required by law, no person shall be recognised by the company as holding any share upon any trust and (except as otherwise provided by the articles or by law) the company shall not be bound by or recognise any interest in any share except an absolute right to the entirety thereof in the holder.

SHARE CERTIFICATES

6. Every member, upon becoming the holder of any shares, shall be entitled without payment to one certificate for all the shares of each class held by him (and, upon transferring a part of his holding of shares of any class, to a certificate for the balance of such holding) or several certificates each for one or more of his shares of any class, to a certificate for the balance of such holding) or several certificates each for one or more of his shares upon payment for every certificate after the first of such reasonable sum as the directors may determine. Every certificate shall be sealed with the seal and shall specify the number, class and distinguishing numbers (if any) of the shares to which it relates and the amount or respective amounts paid up thereon. The company shall not be bound to issue more than one certificate for shares held jointly by several persons and delivery of a certificate to one joint holder shall be a sufficient delivery to all of them.

7. If a share certificate is defaced, worn-out, lost or destroyed, it may be renewed on such terms (if any) as to evidence and indemnity and payment of the expenses reasonably incurred by the company in investigating evidence as the directors may determine but otherwise free of charge, and (in the case of defacement or wearing-out) on delivery up of the old certificate.

LIEN

8. The company shall have a first and paramount lien on every share (not being a fully paid share) for all moneys (whether presently payable or not) payable at a fixed time or called in respect of that share. The directors may at any time declare any share to be wholly or in part exempt from the provisions of this regulation. The company's lien on a share shall extend to any amount payable in respect of it.

9. The company may sell in such manner as the directors determine any shares on which the company has a lien if a sum in respect of which the lien exists is presently payable and is not paid within fourteen clear days after notice has been given to the holder of the share or to the person entitled to it in consequence of the death or bankruptcy of the holder, demanding payment and stating that if the notice is not complied with the shares may be sold.

10. To give effect to a sale the directors may authorise some person to execute an instrument of transfer of the shares sold to, or in accordance with the directions of, the purchaser. The title of the transferee to the shares shall not be affected by any irregularity in or invalidity of the proceedings in reference to the sale.

11. The net proceeds of the sale, after payment of the costs, shall be applied in payment of so much of the sum for which the lien exists as is presently payable, and any residue shall (upon surrender to the company for cancellation of the certificate for the shares sold and subject to a like lien for any moneys not presently payable as existed upon the shares before the sale) be paid to the person entitled to the shares at the date of the sale.

CALLS ON SHARES AND FORFEITURE

12. Subject to the terms of allotment, the directors may make calls upon the members in respect of any moneys unpaid on their shares (whether in respect of nominal value or premium) and each member shall (subject to receiving at least fourteen clear days' notice specifying when and where payment is to be made) pay to the company as required by the notice the amount called on his shares. A call may be required to be paid by instalments. A call may, before receipt by the company of any sum due thereunder, be revoked in whole or part and payment of a call may be postponed in whole or part. A person upon whom a call is made shall remain liable for calls made upon him notwithstanding the subsequent transfer of the shares in respect whereof the call was made.

13. A call shall be deemed to have been made at the time when the resolution of the directors authorising the call was passed.

14. The joint holders of a share shall be jointly and severally liable to pay all calls in respect thereof.

15. If a call remains unpaid after it has become due and payable the person from whom it is due and payable shall pay interest on the amount unpaid from the day it became due and payable until it is paid at the rate fixed by the terms of allotment of the share or in the notice of the call or, if no rate is fixed, at the appropriate rate (as defined by the Act) but the directors may waive payment of the interest wholly or in part.

16. An amount payable in respect of a share on allotment or at any fixed date, whether in respect of nominal value or premium or as an instalment of a call, shall be deemed to be a call and if it is not paid the provisions of the articles shall apply as if that amount had become due and payable by virtue of a call.

17. Subject to the terms of allotment, the directors may make arrangements on the issue of shares for a difference between the holders in the amounts and times of payment of calls on their shares.

18. If a call remains unpaid after it has become due and payable the directors may give to the person from whom it is due not less than fourteen clear days' notice requiring payment of the amount unpaid together with any interest which may have accrued. The notice shall name the place where payment is to be made and shall state that if the notice is not complied with the shares in respect of which the call was made will be liable to be forfeited.

19. If the notice is not complied with any share in respect of which it was given may, before the payment required by the notice has been made, be forfeited by a resolution of the directors and the forfeiture shall include all dividends or other moneys payable in respect of the forfeited shares and not paid before the forfeiture.

20. Subject to the provisions of the Act, a forfeited share may be sold, re-allotted or otherwise disposed of on such terms and in such manner as the directors determine either to the person who was before the forfeiture the holder or to any other person and at any time before sale, re-allotment or other disposition, the forfeiture may be cancelled on such terms as the directors think fit. Where for the purposes of its disposal a forfeited share is to be transferred to any person the directors may authorise some person to execute an instrument of transfer of the share to that person.

21. A person any of whose shares have been forfeited shall cease to be a member in respect of them and shall surrender to the company for cancellation the certificate for the shares forfeited but shall remain liable to the company for all moneys which at the date of forfeiture

were presently payable by him to the company in respect of those shares with interest at the rate at which interest was payable on those moneys before the forfeiture or, if no interest was so payable, at the appropriate rate (as defined in the Act) from the date of forfeiture until payment but the directors may waive payment wholly or in part or enforce payment without any allowance for the value of the shares at the time of forfeiture or for any consideration received on their disposal.

22. A statutory declaration by a director or the secretary that a share has been forfeited on a specified date shall be conclusive evidence of the facts stated in it as against all persons claiming to be entitled to the share and the declaration shall (subject to the execution of an instrument of transfer if necessary) constitute a good title to the share and the person to whom the share is disposed of shall not be bound to see to the application of the consideration, if any, nor shall his title to the share be affected by any irregularity in or invalidity of the proceedings in reference to the forfeiture or disposal of the share.

TRANSFER OF SHARES

23. The instrument of transfer of a share may be in any usual form or in any other form which the directors may approve and shall be executed by or on behalf of the transferor and, unless the share is fully paid, by or on behalf of the transferee.

24. The directors may refuse to register the transfer of a share which is not fully paid to a person of whom they do not approve and they may refuse to register the transfer of a share on which the company has a lien. They may also refuse to register a transfer unless:

    a) it is lodged at the office or at such other place as the directors may appoint and is accompanied by the certificate for the shares to which it relates and such other evidence as the directors may reasonably require to show the right of the transferor to make the transfer;

    b) it is in respect of only one class of shares; and

    c) it is in favour of not more than four transferees.

25. If the directors refuse to register a transfer of a share, they shall within two months after the date on which the transfer was lodged with the company send to the transferee notice of the refusal.

26. The registration of transfers of shares or of transfers of any class of shares may be suspended at such times and for such periods (not exceeding thirty days in any year) as the directors may determine.

27. No fee shall be charged for the registration of any instrument of transfer or other document relating to or affecting the title to any share.

28. The company shall be entitled to retain any instrument of transfer which is registered, but any instrument of transfer which the directors refuse to register shall be returned to the person lodging it when notice of the refusal is given.

TRANSMISSION OF SHARES

29. If a member dies the survivor or survivors where he was a joint holder, and his personal representatives where he was a sole holder or the only survivor of joint holders, shall be the only persons recognised by the company as having any title to his interest; but nothing herein contained shall release the estate of a deceased member from any liability in respect of any share which had been jointly held by him.

30. A person becoming entitled to a share in consequence of the death or bankruptcy of a member may, upon such evidence being produced as the directors may properly require, elect either to become the holder of the share or to have some person nominated by him registered as the transferee. If he elects to become the holder he shall give notice to the company to that effect. If he elects to have another person registered he shall execute an instrument of transfer of the share to that person. All the articles relating to the transfer of shares shall apply to the notice or instrument of transfer as if it were an instrument of transfer executed by the member and the death or bankruptcy of the member had not occurred.

31. A person becoming entitled to a share in consequence of the death or bankruptcy of a member shall have the rights to which he would be entitled if he were the holder of the share, except that he shall not, before being registered as the holder of the share, be entitled in respect of it to attend or vote at any meeting of the company or at any separate meeting of the holders of any class of shares in the company.

ALTERATION OF SHARE CAPITAL

32. The company may by ordinary resolution:
    a) increase its share capital by new shares of such amount as the resolution prescribes;
    b) consolidate and divide all or any of its share capital into shares of larger amount than its existing shares;
    c) subject to the provisions of the Act, sub-divide its shares, or any of them, into shares of smaller amount and the resolution may determine that, as between the shares resulting from the sub-division, any of them may have any preference or advantage as compared with the others; and
    d) cancel shares which, at the date of the passing of the resolution, have not been taken or agreed to be taken by any person and diminish the amount of its share capital by the amount of the shares so cancelled.

33. Whenever as a result of a consolidation of shares any members would become entitled to fractions of a share, the directors may, on behalf of those members, sell the shares representing the fractions for the best price reasonably obtainable to any person (including, subject to the provisions of the Act, the company) and distribute the net proceeds of sale in due proportion among those members, and the directors may authorise some person to execute an instrument of transfer of the shares to, or in accordance with the directions of, the purchaser. The transferee shall not be bound to see to the application of the purchase money nor shall his title to the shares be affected by any irregularity in or invalidity of the proceedings in reference to the sale.

34. Subject to the provisions of the Act, the company may by special resolution reduce its share capital, any capital redemption reserve and any share premium account in any way.

PURCHASE OF OWN SHARES

35. Subject to the provisions of the Act, the company may purchase its own shares (including any redeemable shares) and, if it is a private company, make a payment in respect of the redemption or purchase of its own shares otherwise than out of distributable profits of the company or the proceeds of a fresh issue of shares.

GENERAL MEETINGS

37. The directors may call general meetings and, on the requisition of members pursuant to the provisions of the Act, shall forthwith proceed to convene a general meeting in accordance with the provisions of the Act. If there are not within the United Kingdom sufficient directors to call a general meeting, any director or any member of the company may call a general meeting.

NOTICE OF GENERAL MEETINGS

38. General meetings shall be called by at least fourteen clear days' notice but a general meeting may be called by shorter notice if is so agreed by a majority in number of the members having a right to attend and vote being a majority together holding not less than ninety per cent in nominal value of the shares giving that right.

    The notice shall specify the time and place of the meeting and the general nature of the business to be transacted.

    Subject to the provisions of the articles and to any restrictions imposed on any shares, the notice shall be given to all the members, to all persons entitled to a share in consequence of the death or bankruptcy of a member and to the directors and auditors.

39. The accidental omission to give notice of a meeting to, or the non-receipt of notice of a meeting by, any person entitled to receive notice shall not invalidate the proceedings at that meeting.

PROCEEDINGS AT GENERAL MEETINGS

40. No business shall be transacted at any meeting unless a quorum is present. Save in the case of a company with a single member two persons entitled to vote upon the business to be transacted, each being a member or a proxy for a member or a duly authorised representative of a corporation, shall be a quorum.

41. If such a quorum is not present within half an hour from the time appointed for the meeting, or if during a meeting such a quorum ceases to be present, the meeting shall stand adjourned to the same day in the next week at the same time and place or to such time and place as the directors may determine.

42. The chairman, if any, of the board of directors or in his absence some other director nominated by the directors shall preside as chairman of the meeting, but if neither the chairman nor such other director (if any) be present within fifteen minutes after the time appointed for holding the meeting and willing to act, the directors present shall elect one of their number to be chairman and, if there is only one director present and willing to act, he shall be chairman.

43. If no director is willing to act as chairman, or if no director is present within fifteen minutes after the time appointed for holding the meeting, the members present and entitled to vote shall choose one of their number to be chairman.

44. A director shall, notwithstanding that he is not a member, be entitled to attend and speak at any general meeting and at any separate meeting of the holders of any class of shares in the company.

45. The chairman may, with the consent of a meeting at which a quorum is present (and shall if so directed by the meeting), adjourn the meeting from time to time and from place to place, but no business shall be transacted at an adjourned meeting other than business which might properly have been transacted at the meeting had the adjournment not taken

place. When a meeting is adjourned for fourteen days or more, at least seven clear days' notice shall be given specifying the time and place of the adjourned meeting and the general nature of the business to be transacted. Otherwise it shall not be necessary to give any such notice.

46. A resolution put to the vote of a meeting shall be decided on a show of hands unless before, or on the declaration of the result of, the show of hands a poll is duly demanded. Subject to the provisions of the Act, a poll may be demanded:

   a) by the chairman; or

   b) by at least two members having the right to vote at the meeting; or

   c) by a member or members representing not less than one-tenth of the total voting rights of all the members having the right to vote at the meeting; or

   d) by a member or members holding shares conferring a right to vote at the meeting being shares on which an aggregate sum has been paid up equal to not less than one-tenth of the total sum paid up on all the shares conferring that right;

   and a demand by a person as proxy for a member shall be the same as a demand by the member.

47. Unless a poll is duly demanded a declaration by the chairman that a resolution has been carried or carried unanimously, or by a particular majority, or lost, or not carried by a particular majority and an entry to that effect in the minutes of the meeting shall be conclusive evidence of the fact without proof of the number or proportion of the votes recorded in favour of or against the resolution.

48. The demand for a poll may, before the poll is taken, be withdrawn but only with the consent of the chairman and a demand so withdrawn shall not be taken to have invalidated the result of a show of hands declared before the demand was made.

49. A poll shall be taken as the chairman directs and he may appoint scrutineers (who need not be members) and fix a time and place for declaring the result of the poll. The result of the poll shall be deemed to be the resolution of the meeting at which the poll was demanded.

51. A poll demanded on the election of a chairman or on a question of adjournment shall be taken forthwith. A poll demanded on any other question shall be taken either forthwith or at such time and place as the chairman directs not being more than thirty days after the poll is demanded. The demand for a poll shall not prevent the continuance of a meeting for the transaction of any business other than the question on which the poll was demanded. If a poll is demanded before the declaration of the result of a show of hands and the demand is duly withdrawn, the meeting shall continue as if the demand had not been made.

52. No notice need be given of a poll not taken forthwith if the time and place at which it is to be taken are announced at the meeting at which it is demanded. In any other case at least seven clear days' notice shall be given specifying the time and place at which the poll is to be taken.

VOTES OF MEMBERS

54. Subject to any rights or restrictions attached to any shares, on a show of hands every member who (being an individual) is present in person or by proxy or (being a corporation) is present by a duly authorised representative or by proxy, unless the proxy (in either case) or the representative is himself a member entitled to vote, shall have one vote and on a poll every member shall have one vote for every share of which he is the holder.

55. In the case of joint holders the vote of the senior who tenders a vote, whether in person or by proxy, shall be accepted to the exclusion of the votes of the other joint holders; and seniority shall be determined by the order in which the names of the holders stand in the register of members.

56. A member in respect of whom an order has been made by any court having jurisdiction (whether in the United Kingdom or elsewhere) in matters concerning mental disorder may vote, whether on a show of hands or on a poll, by his receiver, curator bonis or other person authorised in that behalf appointed by that court, and any such receiver, curator bonis or other person may, on a poll, vote by proxy. Evidence to the satisfaction of the directors of the authority of the person claiming to exercise the right to vote shall be deposited at the office, or at such other place as is specified in accordance with the articles for the deposit of instruments of proxy, not less than 48 hours before the time appointed for holding the meeting or adjourned meeting at which the right to vote is to be exercised and in default the right to vote shall not be exercisable.

57. No member shall vote at any general meeting or at any separate meeting of the holders of any class of shares in the company, either in person or by proxy, in respect of any share held by him unless all moneys presently payable by him in respect of that share have been paid.

58. No objection shall be raised to the qualification of any voter except at the meeting or adjourned meeting at which the vote objected to is tendered, and every vote not disallowed at the meeting shall be valid. Any objection made in due time shall be referred to the chairman whose decision shall be final and conclusive.

59. On a poll votes may be given either personally or by proxy. A member may appoint more than one proxy to attend on the same occasion.

60. The appointment of a proxy shall be executed by or on behalf of the appointor and shall be in the following form (or in a form as near thereto as circumstances allow or in any other form which is usual or which the directors may approve):

"........................ PLC/Limited

....

I/We, ..., of ...., being a member/members of the above-named company, hereby appoint .... of ...., or failing him, ... of ...., as my/our proxy to vote in my/our name[s] and on my/our behalf at the general meeting of the company to be held on .... 19............, and at any adjournment thereof.

Signed on .... 19............".

61. Where it is desired to afford members an opportunity of instructing the proxy how he shall act the appointment of a proxy shall be in the following form (or in a form as near thereto as circumstances allow or in any other form which is usual or which the directors may approve):

"...................... PLC/Limited

....

I/We, ..., of ...., being a member/members of the above-named company, hereby appoint .... of ...., or failing him .... of ...., as my/our proxy to vote in my/our name[s] and on my/our behalf at the general meeting of the company, to be held on .... 19............, and at any adjournment thereof.

This form is to be used in respect of the resolutions mentioned below as follows:

Resolution No. 1 *for *against

Resolution No. 2 *for *against.

*Strike out whichever is not desired.

Unless otherwise instructed, the proxy may vote as he thinks fit or abstain from voting.

Signed this .... day of .... 19............".

62. The appointment of a proxy and any authority under which it is executed or a copy of such authority certified notarially or in some other way approved by the directors may:

a) in the case of an instrument in writing be deposited at the office or at such other place within the United Kingdom as is specified in the notice convening the meeting or in any instrument of proxy sent out by the company in relation to the meeting not less than 48 hours before the time for holding the meeting or adjourned meeting at which the person named in the instrument proposes to vote; or

aa) in the case of an appointment contained in an electronic communication, where an address has been specified for the purpose of receiving electronic communications:

ii) in the notice convening the meeting, or

iii) in any instrument of proxy sent out by the company in relation to the meeting, or

iv) in any invitation contained in an electronic communication to appoint a proxy issued by the company in relation to the meeting, be received at such address not less than 48 hours before the time for holding the meeting or adjourned meeting at which the person named in the appointment proposes to vote;

b) in the case of a poll taken more than 48 hours after it is demanded, be deposited or received as aforesaid after the poll has been demanded and not less than 24 hours before the time appointed for the taking of the poll; or

c) where the poll is not taken forthwith but is taken not more than 48 hours after it was demanded, be delivered at the meeting at which the poll was demanded to the chairman or to the secretary or to any director; and an appointment of proxy which is not deposited, delivered or received in a manner so permitted shall be invalid.

In this regulation and the next, "address", in relation to electronic communications, includes any number or address used for the purposes of such communications.

63. A vote given or poll demanded by proxy or by the duly authorised representative of a corporation shall be valid notwithstanding the previous determination of the authority of the person voting or demanding a poll unless notice of the determination was received by the company at the office or at such other place at which the instrument of proxy was duly deposited or, where the appointment of the proxy was contained in an electronic communication, at the address at which such appointment was duly received before the commencement of the meeting or adjourned meeting at which the vote is given or the poll demanded or (in the case of a poll taken otherwise than on the same day as the meeting or adjourned meeting) the time appointed for taking the poll.

NUMBER OF DIRECTORS

64. Unless otherwise determined by ordinary resolution, the number of directors (other than alternate directors) shall not be subject to any maximum but shall be not less than two.

ALTERNATE DIRECTORS

65. Any director (other than an alternate director) may appoint any other director, or any other person approved by resolution of the directors and willing to act, to be an alternate director and may remove from office an alternate director so appointed by him.

66. An alternate director shall be entitled to receive notice of all meetings of directors and of all meetings of committees of directors of which his appointor is a member, to attend and vote at any such meeting at which the director appointing him is not personally present and generally to perform all the functions of his appointor as a director in his absence but shall not be entitled to receive any remuneration from the company for his services as an alternate director. But it shall not be necessary to give notice of such a meeting to an alternate director who is absent from the United Kingdom.

67. An alternate director shall cease to be an alternate director if his appointor ceases to be a director; but, if a director retires by rotation or otherwise but is reappointed or deemed to have been reappointed at the meeting at which he retires, any appointment of an alternate director made by him which was in force immediately prior to his retirement shall continue after his reappointment.

68. Any appointment or removal of an alternate director shall be by notice to the company signed by the director making or revoking the appointment or in any other manner approved by the directors.

69. Save as otherwise provided in the articles, an alternate director shall be deemed for all purposes to be a director and shall alone be responsible for his own acts and defaults and he shall not be deemed to be the agent of the director appointing him.

POWERS OF DIRECTORS

70. Subject to the provisions of the Act, the memorandum and the articles and to any directions given by special resolution, the business of the company shall be managed by the directors who may exercise all the powers of the company. No alteration of the memorandum or articles and no such direction shall invalidate any prior act of the directors which would have been valid if that alteration had not been made or that direction had not been given. The powers given by this regulation shall not be limited by any special power given to the directors by the articles and a meeting of directors at which a quorum is present may exercise all powers exercisable by the directors.

71. The directors may, by power of attorney or otherwise, appoint any person to be the agent of the company for such purposes and on such conditions as they determine, including authority for the agent to delegate all or any of his powers.

DELEGATION OF DIRECTORS' POWERS

72. The directors may delegate any of their powers to any committee consisting of one or more directors. They may also delegate to any managing director or any director holding any other executive office such of their powers as they consider desirable to be exercised by him. Any such delegation may be made subject to any conditions the directors may impose, and either collaterally with or to the exclusion of their own powers and may be revoked or altered. Subject to any such conditions, the proceedings of a committee with two or more members shall be governed by the articles regulating the proceedings of directors so far as they are capable of applying.

APPOINTMENT AND RETIREMENT OF DIRECTORS

76. No person shall be appointed or reappointed a director at any general meeting unless:

    a) he is recommended by the directors; or

    b) not less than fourteen nor more than thirty-five clear days before the date appointed for the meeting, notice executed by a member qualified to vote at the meeting has been given to the company of the intention to propose that person for appointment or reappointment stating the particulars which would, if he were so appointed or reappointed, be required to be included in the company's register of directors together with notice executed by that person of his willingness to be appointed or reappointed.

77. Not less than seven nor more than twenty-eight clear days before the date appointed for holding a general meeting notice shall be given to all who are entitled to receive notice of the meeting of any person who is recommended by the directors for appointment or reappointment as a director at the meeting or in respect of whom notice has been duly given to the company of the intention to propose him at the meeting for appointment or reappointment as a director. The notice shall give the particulars of that person which would, if he were so appointed or reappointed, be required to be included in the company's register of directors.

78. The company may by ordinary resolution appoint a person who is willing to act to be a director either to fill a vacancy or as an additional director and may also determine the rotation in which any additional directors are to retire.

79. The directors may appoint a person who is willing to act to be a director, either to fill a vacancy or as an additional director, provided that the appointment does not cause the number of directors to exceed any number fixed by or in accordance with the articles as the maximum number of directors.

DISQUALIFICATION AND REMOVAL OF DIRECTORS

81. The office of a director shall be vacated if:

    a) he ceases to be a director by virtue of any provision of the Act or he becomes prohibited by law from being a director; or

    b) he becomes bankrupt or makes any arrangement or composition with his creditors generally; or

    c) he is, or may be, suffering from mental disorder and either:

        i) he is admitted to hospital in pursuance of an application for admission for treatment under the Mental Health Act 1983 or, in Scotland, an application for admission under the Mental Health (Scotland) Act 1960, or

        ii) an order is made by a court having jurisdiction (whether in the United Kingdom or elsewhere) in matters concerning mental disorder for his detention or for the appointment of a receiver, curator bonis or other person to exercise powers with respect to his property or affairs; or

    d) he resigns his office by notice to the company; or

    e) he shall for more than six consecutive months have been absent without permission of the directors from meetings of directors held during that period and the directors resolve that his office be vacated.

REMUNERATION OF DIRECTORS

82. The directors shall be entitled to such remuneration as the company may by ordinary resolution determine and, unless the resolution provides otherwise, the remuneration shall be deemed to accrue from day to day.

DIRECTORS' EXPENSES

83. The directors may be paid all travelling, hotel, and other expenses properly incurred by them in connection with their attendance at meetings of directors or committees of directors or general meetings or separate meetings of the holders of any class of shares or of debentures of the company or otherwise in connection with the discharge of their duties.

DIRECTORS' APPOINTMENTS AND INTERESTS

84. Subject to the provisions of the Act, the directors may appoint one or more of their number to the office of managing director or to any other executive office under the company and may enter into an agreement or arrangement with any director for his employment by the company or for the provision by him of any services outside the scope of the ordinary duties of a director. Any such appointment, agreement or arrangement may be made upon such terms as the directors determine and they may remunerate any such director for his services as they think fit. Any appointment of a director to an executive office shall terminate if he ceases to be a director but without prejudice to any claim to damages for breach of the contract of service between the director and the company. A managing director and a director holding any other executive office shall not be subject to retirement by rotation.

85. Subject to the provisions of the Act, and provided that he has disclosed to the directors the nature and extent of any material interest of his, a director notwithstanding his office:

    a) may be a party to, or otherwise interested in, any transaction or arrangement with the company or in which the company or in which the company is otherwise interested;

    b) may be a director or other officer of, or employed by, or a party to any transaction or arrangement with, or otherwise interested in, any body corporate promoted by the company or in which the company is otherwise interested; and

    c) shall not, by reason of his office, be accountable to the company for any benefit which he derives from any such office or employment or from any such transaction or arrangement or from any interest in any such body corporate and no such transaction or arrangement shall be liable to be avoided on the ground of any such interest or benefit.

86. For the purposes of regulation 85:

    a) a general notice given to the directors that a director is to be regarded as having an interest of the nature and extent specified in the notice in any transaction or arrangement in which a specified person or class of persons is interested shall be deemed to be a disclosure that the director has an interest in any such transaction of the nature and extent so specified; and

    b) an interest of which a director has no knowledge and of which it is unreasonable to expect him to have knowledge shall not be treated as an interest of his.

DIRECTORS' GRATUITIES AND PENSIONS

87. The directors may provide benefits, whether by the payment of gratuities or pensions or by insurance or otherwise, for any director who has held but no longer holds any

executive office or employment with the company or with any body corporate which is or has been a subsidiary of the company or a predecessor in business of the company or of any such subsidiary, and for any member of his family (including a spouse and a former spouse) or any person who is or was dependent on him, and may (as well before as after he ceases to hold such office or employment) contribute to any fund and pay premiums for the purchase or provision of any such benefit.

PROCEEDINGS OF DIRECTORS

88. Subject to the provisions of the articles, the directors may regulate their proceedings as they think fit. A director may, and the secretary at the request of a director shall, call a meeting of the directors. It shall not be necessary to give notice of a meeting to a director who is absent from the United Kingdom. Questions arising at a meeting shall be decided by a majority of votes. In the case of an equality of votes, the chairman shall have a second or casting vote. A director who is also an alternate director shall be entitled in the absence of his appointor to a separate vote on behalf of his appointor in addition to his own vote.

89. The quorum for the transaction of the business of the directors may be fixed by the directors and unless so fixed at any other number shall be two. A person who holds office only as an alternate director shall, if his appointor is not present, be counted in the quorum.

90. The continuing directors or a sole continuing director may act notwithstanding any vacancies in their number, but, if the number of directors is less than the number fixed as the quorum, the continuing directors or director may act only for the purpose of filling vacancies or of calling a general meeting.

91. The directors may appoint one of their number to be the chairman of the board of directors and may at any time remove him from that office. Unless he is unwilling to do so, the director so appointed shall preside at every meeting of directors at which he is present. But if there is no director holding that office, or if the director holding it is unwilling to preside or is not present within five minutes after the time appointed for the meeting, the directors present may appoint one of their number to be chairman of the meeting.

92. All acts done by a meeting of directors, or of a committee of directors, or by a person acting as a director shall, notwithstanding that it be afterwards discovered that there was a defect in the appointment of any director or that any of them were disqualified from holding office, or had vacated office, or were not entitled to vote, be as valid as if every such person had been duly appointed and was qualified and had continued to be a director and had been entitled to vote.

93. A resolution in writing signed by all the directors entitled to receive notice of a meeting of directors or of a committee of directors shall be as valid and effectual as it if had been passed at a meeting of directors or (as the case may be) a committee of directors duly convened and held and may consist of several documents in the like form each signed by one or more directors; but a resolution signed by an alternate director need not also be signed by his appointor and, if it is signed by a director who has appointed an alternate director, it need not be signed by the alternate director in that capacity.

94. Save as otherwise provided by the articles, a director shall not vote at a meeting of directors or of a committee of directors on any resolution concerning a matter in which he has, directly or indirectly, an interest or duty which is material and which conflicts or may conflict with the interests of the company unless his interest or duty arises only because the case falls within one or more of the following paragraphs:

a) the resolution relates to the giving to him of a guarantee, security, or indemnity in respect of money lent to, or an obligation incurred by him for the benefit of, the company or any of its subsidiaries;

b) the resolution relates to the giving to a third party of a guarantee, security, or indemnity in respect of an obligation of the company or any of its subsidiaries for which the director has assumed responsibility in whole or part and whether alone or jointly with others under a guarantee or indemnity or by the giving of security;

c) his interest arises by virtue of his subscribing or agreeing to subscribe for any shares, debentures, or other securities of the company or any of its subsidiaries, or by virtue of his being, or intending to become, a participant in the underwriting or sub-underwriting of an offer of any such shares, debentures, or other securities by the company or any of its subsidiaries for subscription, purchase or exchange;

d) the resolution relates in any way to a retirement benefits scheme which has been approved, or is conditional upon approval, by the Board of Inland Revenue for taxation purposes.

For the purposes of this regulation, an interest of a person who is, for any purpose of the Act (excluding any statutory modification thereof not in force when this regulation becomes binding on the company), connected with a director shall be treated as an interest of the director and, in relation to an alternate director, an interest of his appointor shall be treated as an interest of the alternate director without prejudice to any interest which the alternate director has otherwise.

95. A director shall not be counted in the quorum present at a meeting in relation to a resolution on which he is not entitled to vote.

96. The company may by ordinary resolution suspend or relax to any extent, either generally or in respect of any particular matter, any provision of the articles prohibiting a director from voting at a meeting of directors or of a committee of directors.

97. Where proposals are under consideration concerning the appointment of two or more directors to offices or employments with the company or any body corporate in which the company is interested the proposals may be divided and considered in relation to each director separately and (provided he is not for another reason precluded from voting) each of the directors concerned shall be entitled to vote and be counted in the quorum in respect of each resolution except that concerning his own appointment.

98. If a question arises at a meeting of directors or of a committee of directors as to the right of a director to vote, the question may, before the conclusion of the meeting, be referred to the chairman of the meeting and his ruling in relation to any director other than himself shall be final and conclusive.

SECRETARY

99. Subject to the provisions of the Act, the secretary shall be appointed by the directors for such term, at such remuneration and upon such conditions as they may think fit; and any secretary so appointed may be removed by them.

MINUTES

100. The directors shall cause minutes to be made in books kept for the purpose:

a) of all appointments of officers made by the directors; and

b) of all proceedings at meetings of the company, of the holders of any class of shares in the company, and of the directors, and of committees of directors, including the names of the directors present at each such meeting.

THE SEAL

101. The seal shall only be used by the authority of the directors or of a committee of directors authorised by the directors. The directors may determine who shall sign any instrument to which the seal is affixed and unless otherwise so determined it shall be signed by a director and by the secretary or by a second director.

DIVIDENDS

102. Subject to the provisions of the Act, the company may by ordinary resolution declare dividends in accordance with the respective rights of the members, but no dividend shall exceed the amount recommended by the directors.

103. Subject to the provisions of the Act, the directors may pay interim dividends if it appears to them that they are justified by the profits of the company available for distribution. If the share capital is divided into different classes, the directors may pay interim dividends on shares which confer deferred or non-preferred rights with regard to dividend as well as on shares which confer preferential rights with regard to dividend, but no interim dividend shall be paid on shares carrying deferred or non-preferred rights if, at the time of payment, any preferential dividend is in arrear. The directors may also pay at intervals settled by them any dividend payable at a fixed rate if it appears to them that the profits available for distribution justify the payment. Provided the directors act in good faith they shall not incur any liability to the holders of shares conferring preferred rights for any loss they may suffer by the lawful payment of an interim dividend on any shares having deferred or non-preferred rights.

104. Except as otherwise provided by the rights attached to shares, all dividends shall be declared and paid according to the amounts paid up on the shares on which the dividend is paid. All dividends shall be apportioned and paid proportionately to the amounts paid up on the shares during any portion or portions of the period in respect of which the dividend is paid; but, if any share is issued on terms providing that it shall rank for dividend as from a particular date, that share shall rank for dividend accordingly.

105. A general meeting declaring a dividend may, upon the recommendation of the directors, direct that it shall be satisfied wholly or partly by the distribution of assets and, where any difficulty arises in regard to the distribution, the directors may settle the same and in particular may issue fractional certificates and fix the value for distribution of any assets and may determine that cash shall be paid to any member upon the footing of the value so fixed in order to adjust the rights of members and may vest any assets in trustees.

106. Any dividend or other moneys payable in respect of a share may be paid by cheque sent by post to the registered address of the person entitled or, if two or more persons are the holders of the share or are jointly entitled to it by reason of the death or bankruptcy of the holder, to the registered address of that one of those persons who is first named in the register of members or to such person and to such address as the person or persons entitled may in writing direct. Every cheque shall be made payable to the order of the person or persons entitled or to such other person as the person or persons entitled may in writing direct and payment of the cheque shall be a good discharge to the company. Any joint holder or other person jointly entitled to a share as aforesaid may give receipts for any dividend or other moneys payable in respect of the share.

107. No dividend or other moneys payable in respect of a share shall bear interest against the company unless otherwise provided by the rights attached to the share.

108. Any dividend which has remained unclaimed for twelve years from the date when it became due for payment shall, if the directors so resolve, be forfeited and cease to remain owing by the company.

ACCOUNTS

109. No member shall (as such) have any right of inspecting any accounting records or other book or document of the company except as conferred by statute or authorised by the directors or by ordinary resolution of the company.

CAPITALISATION OF PROFITS

110. The directors may with the authority of an ordinary resolution of the company:

a) subject as hereinafter provided, resolve to capitalise any undivided profits of the company not required for paying any preferential dividend (whether or not they are available for distribution) or any sum standing to the credit of the company's share premium account or capital redemption reserve;

b) appropriate the sum resolved to be capitalised to the members who would have been entitled to it if it were distributed by way of dividend and in the same proportions and apply such sum on their behalf either in or towards paying up the amounts, if any, for the time being unpaid on any shares held by them respectively, or in paying up in full unissued shares or debentures of the company of a nominal amount equal to that sum, and allot the shares or debentures credited as fully paid to those members, or as they may direct, in those proportions, or partly in one way and partly in the other: but the share premium account, the capital redemption reserve, and any profits which are not available for distribution may, for the purposes of this regulation, only be applied in paying up unissued shares to be allotted to members credited as fully paid;

c) make such provision by the issue of fractional certificates or by payment in cash or otherwise as they determine in the case of shares or debentures becoming distributable under this regulation in fractions; and

d) authorise any person to enter on behalf of all the members concerned into an agreement with the company providing for the allotment to them respectively, credited as fully paid, of any shares or debentures to which they are entitled upon such capitalisation, any agreement made under such authority being binding on all such members.

NOTICES

111. Any notice to be given to or by any person pursuant to the articles (other than a notice calling a meeting of the directors) shall be in writing or shall be given using electronic communications to an address for the time being notified for that purpose to the person giving the notice.

In this regulation, "address", in relation to electronic communications, includes any number or address used for the purposes of such communications.

112. The company may give any notice to a member either personally or by sending it by post in a prepaid envelope addressed to the member at his registered address or by leaving

it at that address or by giving it using electronic communications to an address for the time being notified to the company by the member. In the case of joint holders of a share, all notices shall be given to the joint holder whose name stands first in the register of members in respect of the joint holding and notice so given shall be sufficient notice to all the joint holders. A member whose registered address is not within the United Kingdom and who gives to the company an address within the United Kingdom at which notices may be given to him, or an address to which notices may be sent using electronic communications, shall be entitled to have notices given to him at that address, but otherwise no such member shall be entitled to receive any notice from the company.

In this regulation and the next, "address", in relation to electronic communications, includes any number or address used for the purposes of such communications.

113. A member present, either in person or by proxy, at any meeting of the company or of the holders of any class of shares in the company shall be deemed to have received notice of the meeting and, where requisite, of the purposes for which it was called.

114. Every person who becomes entitled to a share shall be bound by any notice in respect of that share which, before his name is entered in the register of members, has been duly given to a person from whom he derives his title.

115. Proof that an envelope containing a notice was properly addressed, prepaid and posted shall be conclusive evidence that the notice was given. Proof that a notice contained in an electronic communication was sent in accordance with guidance issued by the Institute of Chartered Secretaries and Administrators shall be conclusive evidence that the notice was given. A notice shall be deemed to be given at the expiration of 48 hours after the envelope containing it was posted or, in the case of a notice contained in an electronic communication, at the expiration of 48 hours after the time it was sent.

116. A notice may be given by the company to the persons entitled to a share in consequence of the death or bankruptcy of a member by sending or delivering it, in any manner authorised by the articles for the giving of notice to a member, addressed to them by name, or by the title of representatives of the deceased, or trustee of the bankrupt or by any like description at the address, if any, within the United Kingdom supplied for that purpose by the persons claiming to be so entitled. Until such an address has been supplied, a notice may be given in any manner in which it might have been given if the death or bankruptcy had not occurred.

WINDING UP

117. If the company is wound up, the liquidator may, with the sanction of a special resolution of the company and any other sanction required by the Act, divide among the members in specie the whole or any part of the assets of the company and may, for that purpose, value any assets and determine how the division shall be carried out as between the members or different classes of members. The liquidator may, with the like sanction, vest the whole or any part of the assets in trustees upon such trusts for the benefit of the members as he with the like sanction determines, but no member shall be compelled to accept any assets upon which there is a liability.

INDEMNITY

118. Subject to the provisions of the Act but without prejudice to any indemnity to which a director may otherwise be entitled, every director or other officer or auditor of the company

shall be indemnified out of the assets of the company against any liability incurred by him in defending any proceedings, whether civil or criminal, in which judgment is given in his favour or in which he is acquitted or in connection with any application in which relief is granted to him by the court from liability for negligence, default, breach of duty or breach of trust in relation to the affairs of the company.

APPENDIX D
Table C to the Companies Act 1985 as amended by SI 2007/2541 and SI 2007/2826

REGULATIONS FOR MANAGEMENT OF A COMPANY LIMITED BY GUARANTEE AND NOT HAVING A SHARE CAPITAL

VERSION IN FORCE FROM 1ST OCTOBER 2007 TO 30TH SEPTEMBER 2009

PRELIMINARY

A1. References in these Articles to Table A are to that Table so far as it relates to private companies limited by shares.

1. Regulations 2 to 35 inclusive, 54, 55, 57, 59, 102 to 108 inclusive, 110, 114, 116 and 117 of Table A, shall not apply to the company but the articles hereinafter contained and, subject to the modifications hereinafter expressed, the remaining regulations of Table A shall constitute the articles of association of the company.

INTERPRETATION

2. In regulation 1 of Table A, the definition of "the holder " shall be omitted.

MEMBERS

3. The subscribers to the memorandum of association of the company and such other persons as are admitted to membership in accordance with the articles shall be members of the company. No person shall be admitted a member of the company unless he is approved by the directors. Every person who wishes to become a member shall deliver to the company an application for membership in such form as the directors require executed by him.

4. A member may at any time withdraw from the company by giving at least seven clear days' notice to the company. Membership shall not be transferable and shall cease on death.

NOTICE OF GENERAL MEETINGS

5. In regulation 38 of Table A:

   in paragraph (b) the words "of the total voting rights at the meeting of all the members" shall be substituted for "in nominal value of the shares giving that right" and the words "The notice shall be given to all the members and to the directors and auditors" shall be substituted for the last sentence.

PROCEEDINGS AT GENERAL MEETINGS

6. The words "and at any separate meeting of the holders of any class of shares in the company" shall be omitted from regulation 44 of Table A.

7. Paragraph (d) of regulation 46 of Table A shall be omitted.

VOTES OF MEMBERS

8. On a show of hands every member present in person shall have one vote. On a poll every member present in person or by proxy shall have one vote.

DIRECTORS' EXPENSES

9. The words "of any class of shares or" shall be omitted from regulation 83 of Table A.

PROCEEDINGS OF DIRECTORS

10. In paragraph (c) of regulation 94 of Table A the word "debentures" shall be substituted for the words "shares, debentures or other securities" in both places where they occur.

MINUTES

11. The words "of the holders of any class of shares in the company" shall be omitted from regulation 100 of Table A.

NOTICES

12. The second sentence of regulation 112 of Table A shall be omitted.

13. The words "or of the holders of any class of shares in the company" shall be omitted from regulation 113 of Table A.

APPENDIX E
Model articles for private companies limited by shares

INDEX TO THE ARTICLES

PART 1: INTERPRETATION AND LIMITATION OF LIABILITY

PART 2: DIRECTORS
DIRECTORS' POWERS AND RESPONSIBILITIES

DECISION-MAKING BY DIRECTORS

APPOINTMENT OF DIRECTORS

PART 3: SHARES AND DISTRIBUTIONS
SHARES

50. No right to inspect accounts and other records

51. Provision for employees on cessation of business

DIRECTORS' INDEMNITY AND INSURANCE

52. Indemnity

53. Insurance

PART 1: INTERPRETATION AND LIMITATION OF LIABILITY

Defined terms

1. In the articles, unless the context requires otherwise:
   - "articles" means the company's articles of association;
   - "bankruptcy" includes individual insolvency proceedings in a jurisdiction other than England and Wales and Northern Ireland which have an effect similar to that of bankruptcy;
   - "chairman" has the meaning given in article 12;
   - "chairman of the meeting" has the meaning given in article 39;
   - "Companies Acts" means the Companies Acts (as defined in section 2 of the Companies Act 2006), in so far as they apply to the company;
   - "director" means a director of the company, and includes any person occupying the position of director, by whatever name called;
   - "distribution recipient" has the meaning given in article 31;
   - "document" includes, unless otherwise specified, any document sent or supplied in electronic form;
   - "electronic form" has the meaning given in section 1168 of the Companies Act 2006;
   - "fully paid" in relation to a share, means that the nominal value and any premium to be paid to the company in respect of that share have been paid to the company;
   - "hard copy form" has the meaning given in section 1168 of the Companies Act 2006;
   - "holder" in relation to shares means the person whose name is entered in the register of members as the holder of the shares;
   - "instrument" means a document in hard copy form;
   - "ordinary resolution" has the meaning given in section 282 of the Companies Act 2006;
   - "paid" means paid or credited as paid;
   - "participate", in relation to a directors' meeting, has the meaning given in article 45;
   - "proxy notice" has the meaning given in article 45;
   - "shareholder" means a person who is the holder of a share;
   - "shares" means shares in the company;
   - "special resolution" has the meaning given in section 283 of the Companies Act 2006;
   - "subsidiary" has the meaning given in section 1159 of the Companies Act 2006;
   - "transmittee" means a person entitled to a share by reason of the death or bankruptcy of a shareholder or otherwise by operation of law; and
   - "writing" means the representation or reproduction of words, symbols or other information in a visible form by any method or combination of methods, whether sent or supplied in electronic form or otherwise.

Unless the context otherwise requires, other words or expressions contained in these articles bear the same meaning as in the Companies Act 2006 as in force on the date when these articles become binding on the company.

LIABILITY OF MEMBERS

2. The liability of the members is limited to the amount, if any, unpaid on the shares held by them.

PART 2: DIRECTORS
DIRECTORS' POWERS AND RESPONSIBILITIES

Directors' general authority

3. Subject to the articles, the directors are responsible for the management of the company's business, for which purpose they may exercise all the powers of the company.

Shareholders' reserve power

4. (1) The shareholders may, by special resolution, direct the directors to take, or refrain from taking, specified action.

(2) No such special resolution invalidates anything which the directors have done before the passing of the resolution.

Directors may delegate

5. (1) Subject to the articles, the directors may delegate any of the powers which are conferred on them under the articles

a) to such person or committee;

b) by such means (including by power of attorney);

c) to such an extent;

d) in relation to such matters or territories; and

e) on such terms and conditions;

as they think fit.

(2) If the directors so specify, any such delegation may authorise further delegation of the directors' powers by any person to whom they are delegated.

(3) The directors may revoke any delegation in whole or part, or alter its terms and conditions.

Committees

6. (1) Committees to which the directors delegate any of their powers must follow procedures which are based as far as they are applicable on those provisions of the articles which govern the taking of decisions by directors.

(2) The directors may make rules of procedure for all or any committees, which prevail over rules derived from the articles if they are not consistent with them.

DECISION-MAKING BY DIRECTORS

Directors to take decisions collectively

7. (1) The general rule about decision-making by directors is that any decision of the directors must be either a majority decision at a meeting or a decision taken in accordance with article 8.

(2) If:

a) the company only has one director, and

b) no provision of the articles requires it to have more than one director,

the general rule does not apply, and the director may take decisions without regard to any of the provisions of the articles relating to directors' decision-making.

Unanimous decisions

8. (1) A decision of the directors is taken in accordance with this article when all eligible directors indicate to each other by any means that they share a common view on a matter.

(2) Such a decision may take the form of a resolution in writing, copies of which have been signed by each eligible director or to which each eligible director has otherwise indicated agreement in writing.

(3) References in this article to eligible directors are to directors who would have been entitled to vote on the matter had it been proposed as a resolution at a directors' meeting.

(4) A decision may not be taken in accordance with this article if the eligible directors would not have formed a quorum at such a meeting.

Calling a directors' meeting

9. (1) Any director may call a directors' meeting by giving notice of the meeting to the directors or by authorising the company secretary (if any) to give such notice.

(2) Notice of any directors' meeting must indicate:

a) its proposed date and time;

b) where it is to take place; and

c) if it is anticipated that directors participating in the meeting will not be in the same place, how it is proposed that they should communicate with each other during the meeting.

(3) Notice of a directors' meeting must be given to each director, but need not be in writing.

(4) Notice of a directors' meeting need not be given to directors who waive their entitlement to notice of that meeting, by giving notice to that effect to the company not more than 7 days after the date on which the meeting is held. Where such notice is given after the meeting has been held, that does not affect the validity of the meeting, or of any business conducted at it.

Participation in directors' meetings

10. (1) Subject to the articles, directors participate in a directors' meeting, or part of a directors' meeting, when:

a) the meeting has been called and takes place in accordance with the articles, and

b) they can each communicate to the others any information or opinions they have on any particular item of the business of the meeting.

(2) In determining whether directors are participating in a directors' meeting, it is irrelevant where any director is or how they communicate with each other.

(3) If all the directors participating in a meeting are not in the same place, they may decide that the meeting is to be treated as taking place wherever any of them is.

Quorum for directors' meetings

11. (1) At a directors' meeting, unless a quorum is participating, no proposal is to be voted on, except a proposal to call another meeting.

(2) The quorum for directors' meetings may be fixed from time to time by a decision of the directors, but it must never be less than two, and unless otherwise fixed it is two.

(3) If the total number of directors for the time being is less than the quorum required, the directors must not take any decision other than a decision:

a) to appoint further directors, or

b) to call a general meeting so as to enable the shareholders to appoint further directors.

Chairing of directors' meetings

12. (1) The directors may appoint a director to chair their meetings.

(2) The person so appointed for the time being is known as the chairman.

(3) The directors may terminate the chairman's appointment at any time.

(4) If the chairman is not participating in a directors' meeting within ten minutes of the time at which it was to start, the participating directors must appoint one of themselves to chair it.

Casting vote

13. (1) If the numbers of votes for and against a proposal are equal, the chairman or other director chairing the meeting has a casting vote.

(2) But this does not apply if, in accordance with the articles, the chairman or other director is not to be counted as participating in the decision-making process for quorum, or voting purposes.

Conflicts of interest

14. (1) If a proposed decision of the directors is concerned with an actual or proposed transaction or arrangement with the company in which a director is interested, that director is not to be counted as participating in the decision-making process for quorum or voting purposes.

(2) But if paragraph (3) applies, a director who is interested in an actual or proposed transaction or arrangement with the company is to be counted as participating in the decision-making process for quorum and voting purposes.

(3) This paragraph applies when:

a) the company by ordinary resolution disapplies the provision of the articles which would otherwise prevent a director from being counted as participating in the decision-making process;

b) the director's interest cannot reasonably be regarded as likely to give rise to a conflict of interest; or

c) the director's conflict of interest arises from a permitted cause.

(4) For the purposes of this article, the following are permitted causes:

a) a guarantee given, or to be given, by or to a director in respect of an obligation incurred by or on behalf of the company or any of its subsidiaries;

b) subscription, or an agreement to subscribe, for shares or other securities of the company or any of its subsidiaries, or to underwrite, sub-underwrite, or guarantee subscription for any such shares or securities; and

c) arrangements pursuant to which benefits are made available to employees and directors or former employees and directors of the company or any of its subsidiaries which do not provide special benefits for directors or former directors.

(5) For the purposes of this article, references to proposed decisions and decision-making processes include any directors' meeting or part of a directors' meeting.

(6) Subject to paragraph (7), if a question arises at a meeting of directors or of a committee of directors as to the right of a director to participate in the meeting (or part of the meeting) for voting or quorum purposes, the question may, before the conclusion of the meeting, be referred to the chairman whose ruling in relation to any director other than the chairman is to be final and conclusive.

(7) If any question as to the right to participate in the meeting (or part of the meeting) should arise in respect of the chairman, the question is to be decided by a decision of the directors at that meeting, for which purpose the chairman of the meeting is not to be counted as participating in the meeting (or that part of the meeting) for voting or quorum purposes.

Records of decisions to be kept

15. The directors must ensure that the company keeps a record, in writing, for at least 10 years from the date of the decision recorded, of every unanimous or majority decision taken by the directors.

Directors' discretion to make further rules

16. Subject to the articles, the directors may make any rule which they think fit about how they take decisions, and about how such rules are to be recorded or communicated to directors.

APPOINTMENT OF DIRECTORS

Methods of appointing directors

17. (1) Any person who is willing to act as a director, and is permitted by law to do so, may be appointed to be a director:

a) by ordinary resolution, or

b) by a decision of the directors.

(2) In any case where, as a result of death, the company has no shareholders and no directors, the personal representatives of the last shareholder to have died have the right, by notice in writing, to appoint a person to be a director.

(3) For the purposes of paragraph (2), where 2 or more shareholders die in circumstances rendering it uncertain who was the last to die, a younger shareholder is deemed to have survived an older shareholder.

Termination of director's appointment

18. A person ceases to be a director as soon as:

a) that person ceases to be a director by virtue of any provision of the Companies Act 2006 or is prohibited from being a director by law;

b) a bankruptcy order is made against that person;

c) a composition is made with that person's creditors generally in satisfaction of that person's debts;

d) a registered medical practitioner who is treating that person gives a written opinion to the company stating that that person has become physically or mentally incapable of acting as a director and may remain so for more than three months;

e) by reason of that person's mental health, a court makes an order which wholly or partly prevents that person from personally exercising any powers or rights which that person would otherwise have;

f) notification is received by the company from the director that the director is resigning or retiring from office, and such resignation or retirement has taken effect in accordance with its terms.

Directors' remuneration

19. (1) Directors may undertake any services for the company that the directors decide.

(2) Directors are entitled to such remuneration as the directors determine:

a) for their services to the company as directors, and

b) for any other service which they undertake for the company.

(3) Subject to the articles, a director's remuneration may:

a) take any form, and

b) include any arrangements in connection with the payment of a pension, allowance or gratuity, or any death, sickness or disability benefits, to or in respect of that director.

(4) Unless the directors decide otherwise, directors' remuneration accrues from day to day.

(5) Unless the directors decide otherwise, directors are not accountable to the company for any remuneration which they receive as directors or other officers or employees of the company's subsidiaries or of any other body corporate in which the company is interested.

Directors' expenses

20. The company may pay any reasonable expenses which the directors properly incur in connection with their attendance at:

a) meetings of directors or committees of directors,

b) general meetings, or

c) separate meetings of the holders of any class of shares or of debentures of the company,

or otherwise in connection with the exercise of their powers and the discharge of their responsibilities in relation to the company.

PART 3: SHARES AND DISTRIBUTIONS SHARES

All shares to be fully paid up

21. (1) No share is to be issued for less than the aggregate of its nominal value and any premium to be paid to the company in consideration for its issue.

(2) This does not apply to shares taken on the formation of the company by the subscribers to the company's memorandum.

Powers to issue different classes of share

22. (1) Subject to the articles, but without prejudice to the rights attached to any existing share, the company may issue shares with such rights or restrictions as may be determined by ordinary resolution.

(2) The company may issue shares which are to be redeemed, or are liable to be redeemed at the option of the company or the holder, and the directors may determine the terms, conditions and manner of redemption of any such shares.

Company not bound by less than absolute interests

23. Except as required by law, no person is to be recognised by the company as holding any share upon any trust, and except as otherwise required by law or the articles, the company is not in any way to be bound by or recognise any interest in a share other than the holder's absolute ownership of it and all the rights attaching to it.

Share certificates

24. (1) The company must issue each shareholder, free of charge, with one or more certificates in respect of the shares which that shareholder holds.

(2) Every certificate must specify:

a) in respect of how many shares, of what class, it is issued;

b) the nominal value of those shares;

c) that the shares are fully paid; and

d) any distinguishing numbers assigned to them.

(3) No certificate may be issued in respect of shares of more than one class.

(4) If more than one person holds a share, only one certificate may be issued in respect of it.

(5) Certificates must:

a) have affixed to them the company's common seal, or

b) be otherwise executed in accordance with the Companies Acts.

Replacement share certificates

25. (1) If a certificate issued in respect of a shareholder's shares is:

a) damaged or defaced, or

b) said to be lost, stolen or destroyed,

that shareholder is entitled to be issued with a replacement certificate in respect of the same shares.

(2) A shareholder exercising the right to be issued with such a replacement certificate:

a) may at the same time exercise the right to be issued with a single certificate or separate certificates;

b) must return the certificate which is to be replaced to the company if it is damaged or defaced; and

c) must comply with such conditions as to evidence, indemnity and the payment of a reasonable fee as the directors decide.

Share transfers

26. (1) Shares may be transferred by means of an instrument of transfer in any usual form or any other form approved by the directors, which is executed by or on behalf of the transferor.

(2) No fee may be charged for registering any instrument of transfer or other document relating to or affecting the title to any share.

(3) The company may retain any instrument of transfer which is registered.

(4) The transferor remains the holder of a share until the transferee's name is entered in the register of members as holder of it.

(5) The directors may refuse to register the transfer of a share, and if they do so, the instrument of transfer must be returned to the transferee with the notice of refusal unless they suspect that the proposed transfer may be fraudulent.

Transmission of shares

27. (1) If title to a share passes to a transmittee, the company may only recognise the transmittee as having any title to that share.

(2) A transmittee who produces such evidence of entitlement to shares as the directors may properly require:

a) may, subject to the articles, choose either to become the holder of those shares or to have them transferred to another person, and

b) subject to the articles, and pending any transfer of the shares to another person, has the same rights as the holder had.

(3) But transmittees do not have the right to attend or vote at a general meeting, or agree to a proposed written resolution, in respect of shares to which they are entitled, by reason of the holder's death or bankruptcy or otherwise, unless they become the holders of those shares.

Exercise of transmittees' rights

28. (1) Transmittees who wish to become the holders of shares to which they have become entitled must notify the company in writing of that wish.

(2) If the transmittee wishes to have a share transferred to another person, the transmittee must execute an instrument of transfer in respect of it.

(3) Any transfer made or executed under this article is to be treated as if it were made or executed by the person from whom the transmittee has derived rights in respect of the share, and as if the event which gave rise to the transmission had not occurred.

Transmittees bound by prior notices

29. If a notice is given to a shareholder in respect of shares and a transmittee is entitled to those shares, the transmittee is bound by the notice if it was given to the shareholder before the transmittee's name has been entered in the register of members.

DIVIDENDS AND OTHER DISTRIBUTIONS

Procedure for declaring dividends

30. (1) The company may by ordinary resolution declare dividends, and the directors may decide to pay interim dividends.

(2) A dividend must not be declared unless the directors have made a recommendation as to its amount. Such a dividend must not exceed the amount recommended by the directors.

(3) No dividend may be declared or paid unless it is in accordance with shareholders' respective rights.

(4) Unless the shareholders' resolution to declare or directors' decision to pay a dividend, or the terms on which shares are issued, specify otherwise, it must be paid by reference to each shareholder's holding of shares on the date of the resolution or decision to declare or pay it.

(5) If the company's share capital is divided into different classes, no interim dividend may be paid on shares carrying deferred or non-preferred rights if, at the time of payment, any preferential dividend is in arrear.

(6) The directors may pay at intervals any dividend payable at a fixed rate if it appears to them that the profits available for distribution justify the payment.

(7) If the directors act in good faith, they do not incur any liability to the holders of shares conferring preferred rights for any loss they may suffer by the lawful payment of an interim dividend on shares with deferred or non-preferred rights.

Payment of dividends and other distributions

31. (1) Where a dividend or other sum which is a distribution is payable in respect of a share, it must be paid by one or more of the following means:

a) transfer to a bank or building society account specified by the distribution recipient either in writing or as the directors may otherwise decide;

b) sending a cheque made payable to the distribution recipient by post to the distribution recipient at the distribution recipient's registered address (if the distribution recipient is a holder of the share), or (in any other case) to an address specified by the distribution recipient either in writing or as the directors may otherwise decide;

c) sending a cheque made payable to such person by post to such person at such address as the distribution recipient has specified either in writing or as the directors may otherwise decide; or

d) any other means of payment as the directors agree with the distribution recipient either in writing or by such other means as the directors decide.

(2) In the articles, "the distribution recipient" means, in respect of a share in respect of which a dividend or other sum is payable:

a) the holder of the share; or

b) if the share has two or more joint holders, whichever of them is named first in the register of members; or

c) if the holder is no longer entitled to the share by reason of death or bankruptcy, or otherwise by operation of law, the transmittee.

No interest on distributions

32. The company may not pay interest on any dividend or other sum payable in respect of a share unless otherwise provided by:

    a) the terms on which the share was issued, or

    b) the provisions of another agreement between the holder of that share and the company.

Unclaimed distributions

33. (1) All dividends or other sums which are:

    a) payable in respect of shares, and

    b) unclaimed after having been declared or become payable,

    may be invested or otherwise made use of by the directors for the benefit of the company until claimed.

    (2) The payment of any such dividend or other sum into a separate account does not make the company a trustee in respect of it.

    (3) If:

    a) twelve years have passed from the date on which a dividend or other sum became due for payment, and

    b) the distribution recipient has not claimed it,

    the distribution recipient is no longer entitled to that dividend or other sum and it ceases to remain owing by the company.

Non-cash distributions

34. (1) Subject to the terms of issue of the share in question, the company may, by ordinary resolution on the recommendation of the directors, decide to pay all or part of a dividend or other distribution payable in respect of a share by transferring non-cash assets of equivalent value (including, without limitation, shares or other securities in any company).

    (2) For the purposes of paying a non-cash distribution, the directors may make whatever arrangements they think fit, including, where any difficulty arises regarding the distribution:

    a) fixing the value of any assets;

    b) paying cash to any distribution recipient on the basis of that value in order to adjust the rights of recipients; and

    c) vesting any assets in trustees.

Waiver of distributions

35. Distribution recipients may waive their entitlement to a dividend or other distribution payable in respect of a share by giving the company notice in writing to that effect, but if:

    a) the share has more than one holder, or

    b) more than one person is entitled to the share, whether by reason of the death or bankruptcy of one or more joint holders, or otherwise,

    the notice is not effective unless it is expressed to be given, and signed, by all the holders or persons otherwise entitled to the share.

CAPITALISATION OF PROFITS

Authority to capitalise and appropriation of capitalised sums

36. (1) Subject to the articles, the directors may, if they are so authorised by an ordinary resolution:

a) decide to capitalise any profits of the company (whether or not they are available for distribution) which are not required for paying a preferential dividend, or any sum standing to the credit of the company's share premium account or capital redemption reserve; and

b) appropriate any sum which they so decide to capitalise (a "capitalised sum") to the persons who would have been entitled to it if it were distributed by way of dividend (the "persons entitled") and in the same proportions.

(2) Capitalised sums must be applied:

a) on behalf of the persons entitled, and

b) in the same proportions as a dividend would have been distributed to them.

(3) Any capitalised sum may be applied in paying up new shares of a nominal amount equal to the capitalised sum which are then allotted credited as fully paid to the persons entitled or as they may direct.

(4) A capitalised sum which was appropriated from profits available for distribution may be applied in paying up new debentures of the company which are then allotted credited as fully paid to the persons entitled or as they may direct.

(5) Subject to the articles the directors may:

a) apply capitalised sums in accordance with paragraphs (3) and (4) partly in one way and partly in another;

b) make such arrangements as they think fit to deal with shares or debentures becoming distributable in fractions under this article (including the issuing of fractional certificates or the making of cash payments); and

c) authorise any person to enter into an agreement with the company on behalf of all the persons entitled which is binding on them in respect of the allotment of shares and debentures to them under this article.

PART 4: DECISION-MAKING BY SHAREHOLDERS ORGANISATION OF GENERAL MEETINGS

Attendance and speaking at general meetings

37. (1) A person is able to exercise the right to speak at a general meeting when that person is in a position to communicate to all those attending the meeting, during the meeting, any information or opinions which that person has on the business of the meeting.

(2) A person is able to exercise the right to vote at a general meeting when:

a) that person is able to vote, during the meeting, on resolutions put to the vote at the meeting, and

b) that person's vote can be taken into account in determining whether or not such resolutions are passed at the same time as the votes of all the other persons attending the meeting.

(3) The directors may make whatever arrangements they consider appropriate to enable those attending a general meeting to exercise their rights to speak or vote at it.

(4) In determining attendance at a general meeting, it is immaterial whether any two or more members attending it are in the same place as each other.

(5) Two or more persons who are not in the same place as each other attend a general meeting if their circumstances are such that if they have (or were to have) rights to speak and vote at that meeting, they are (or would be) able to exercise them.

Quorum for general meetings

38. No business other than the appointment of the chairman of the meeting is to be transacted at a general meeting if the persons attending it do not constitute a quorum.

Chairing general meetings

39. (1) If the directors have appointed a chairman, the chairman shall chair general meetings if present and willing to do so.

(2) If the directors have not appointed a chairman, or if the chairman is unwilling to chair the meeting or is not present within ten minutes of the time at which a meeting was due to start:

a) the directors present, or

b) (if no directors are present), the meeting,

must appoint a director or shareholder to chair the meeting, and the appointment of the chairman of the meeting must be the first business of the meeting.

(3) The person chairing a meeting in accordance with this article is referred to as "the chairman of the meeting".

Attendance and speaking by directors and non-shareholders

40. (1) Directors may attend and speak at general meetings, whether or not they are shareholders.

(2) The chairman of the meeting may permit other persons who are not:

a) shareholders of the company, or

b) otherwise entitled to exercise the rights of shareholders in relation to general meetings,

to attend and speak at a general meeting.

Adjournment

41. (1) If the persons attending a general meeting within half an hour of the time at which the meeting was due to start do not constitute a quorum, or if during a meeting a quorum ceases to be present, the chairman of the meeting must adjourn it.

(2) The chairman of the meeting may adjourn a general meeting at which a quorum is present if:

a) the meeting consents to an adjournment, or

b) it appears to the chairman of the meeting that an adjournment is necessary to protect the safety of any person attending the meeting or ensure that the business of the meeting is conducted in an orderly manner.

(3) The chairman of the meeting must adjourn a general meeting if directed to do so by the meeting.

(4) When adjourning a general meeting, the chairman of the meeting must:

a) either specify the time and place to which it is adjourned or state that it is to continue at a time and place to be fixed by the directors, and

b) have regard to any directions as to the time and place of any adjournment which have been given by the meeting.

(5) If the continuation of an adjourned meeting is to take place more than 14 days after it was adjourned, the company must give at least 7 clear days' notice of it (that is, excluding the day of the adjourned meeting and the day on which the notice is given):

a) to the same persons to whom notice of the company's general meetings is required to be given, and

b) containing the same information which such notice is required to contain.

(6) No business may be transacted at an adjourned general meeting which could not properly have been transacted at the meeting if the adjournment had not taken place.

VOTING AT GENERAL MEETINGS

Voting: general

42. A resolution put to the vote of a general meeting must be decided on a show of hands unless a poll is duly demanded in accordance with the articles.

Errors and disputes

43. (1) No objection may be raised to the qualification of any person voting at a general meeting except at the meeting or adjourned meeting at which the vote objected to is tendered, and every vote not disallowed at the meeting is valid.

(2) Any such objection must be referred to the chairman of the meeting, whose decision is final.

Poll votes

44. (1) A poll on a resolution may be demanded:

a) in advance of the general meeting where it is to be put to the vote, or

b) at a general meeting, either before a show of hands on that resolution or immediately after the result of a show of hands on that resolution is declared.

(2) A poll may be demanded by:

a) the chairman of the meeting;

b) the directors;

c) two or more persons having the right to vote on the resolution; or

d) a person or persons representing not less than one tenth of the total voting rights of all the shareholders having the right to vote on the resolution.

(3) A demand for a poll may be withdrawn if:

a) the poll has not yet been taken, and

b) the chairman of the meeting consents to the withdrawal.

(4) Polls must be taken immediately and in such manner as the chairman of the meeting directs.

Content of proxy notices

45. (1) Proxies may only validly be appointed by a notice in writing (a "proxy notice") which:

a) states the name and address of the shareholder appointing the proxy;

b) identifies the person appointed to be that shareholder's proxy and the general meeting in relation to which that person is appointed;

c) is signed by or on behalf of the shareholder appointing the proxy, or is authenticated in such manner as the directors may determine; and

d) is delivered to the company in accordance with the articles and any instructions contained in the notice of the general meeting to which they relate.

(2) The company may require proxy notices to be delivered in a particular form, and may specify different forms for different purposes.

(3) Proxy notices may specify how the proxy appointed under them is to vote (or that the proxy is to abstain from voting) on one or more resolutions.

(4) Unless a proxy notice indicates otherwise, it must be treated as:

a) allowing the person appointed under it as a proxy discretion as to how to vote on any ancillary or procedural resolutions put to the meeting, and

b) appointing that person as a proxy in relation to any adjournment of the general meeting to which it relates as well as the meeting itself.

Delivery of proxy notices

46. (1) A person who is entitled to attend, speak or vote (either on a show of hands or on a poll) at a general meeting remains so entitled in respect of that meeting or any adjournment of it, even though a valid proxy notice has been delivered to the company by or on behalf of that person.

(2) An appointment under a proxy notice may be revoked by delivering to the company a notice in writing given by or on behalf of the person by whom or on whose behalf the proxy notice was given.

(3) A notice revoking a proxy appointment only takes effect if it is delivered before the start of the meeting or adjourned meeting to which it relates.

(4) If a proxy notice is not executed by the person appointing the proxy, it must be accompanied by written evidence of the authority of the person who executed it to execute it on the appointor's behalf.

Amendments to resolutions

47. (1) An ordinary resolution to be proposed at a general meeting may be amended by ordinary resolution if:

a) notice of the proposed amendment is given to the company in writing by a person entitled to vote at the general meeting at which it is to be proposed not less than 48 hours before the meeting is to take place (or such later time as the chairman of the meeting may determine), and

b) the proposed amendment does not, in the reasonable opinion of the chairman of the meeting, materially alter the scope of the resolution.

(2) A special resolution to be proposed at a general meeting may be amended by ordinary resolution, if:

a) the chairman of the meeting proposes the amendment at the general meeting at which the resolution is to be proposed, and

b) the amendment does not go beyond what is necessary to correct a grammatical or other non-substantive error in the resolution.

(3) If the chairman of the meeting, acting in good faith, wrongly decides that an amendment to a resolution is out of order, the chairman's error does not invalidate the vote on that resolution.

PART 5: ADMINISTRATIVE ARRANGEMENTS

Means of communication to be used

48. (1) Subject to the articles, anything sent or supplied by or to the company under the articles may be sent or supplied in any way in which the Companies Act 2006 provides for documents or information which are authorised or required by any provision of that Act to be sent or supplied by or to the company.

(2) Subject to the articles, any notice or document to be sent or supplied to a director in connection with the taking of decisions by directors may also be sent or supplied by the means by which that director has asked to be sent or supplied with such notices or documents for the time being.

(3) A director may agree with the company that notices or documents sent to that director in a particular way are to be deemed to have been received within a specified time of their being sent, and for the specified time to be less than 48 hours.

Company seals

49. (1) Any common seal may only be used by the authority of the directors.

(2) The directors may decide by what means and in what form any common seal is to be used.

(3) Unless otherwise decided by the directors, if the company has a common seal and it is affixed to a document, the document must also be signed by at least one authorised person in the presence of a witness who attests the signature.

(4) For the purposes of this article, an authorised person is:

a) any director of the company;

b) the company secretary (if any); or

c) any person authorised by the directors for the purpose of signing documents to which the common seal is applied.

No right to inspect accounts and other records

50. Except as provided by law or authorised by the directors or an ordinary resolution of the company, no person is entitled to inspect any of the company's accounting or other records or documents merely by virtue of being a shareholder.

Provision for employees on cessation of business

51. The directors may decide to make provision for the benefit of persons employed or formerly employed by the company or any of its subsidiaries (other than a director or former director or shadow director) in connection with the cessation or transfer to any person of the whole or part of the undertaking of the company or that subsidiary.

DIRECTORS' INDEMNITY AND INSURANCE

Indemnity

52. (1) Subject to paragraph (2), a relevant officer of the company or an associated company may be indemnified out of the company's assets against:

a) any liability incurred by that director in connection with any negligence, default, breach of duty or breach of trust in relation to the company or an associated company,

b) any liability incurred by that director in connection with the activities of the company or an associated company in its capacity as a trustee of an occupational pension scheme (as defined in section 235(6) of the Companies Act 2006),

c) any other liability incurred by that director as an officer of the company or an associated company.

(2) This article does not authorise any indemnity which would be prohibited or rendered void by any provision of the Companies Acts or by any other provision of law.

(3) In this article:

a) companies are associated if one is a subsidiary of the other or both are subsidiaries of the same body corporate, and

b) a "relevant director" means any director or former director of the company or an associated company.

Insurance

53. (1) The directors may decide to purchase and maintain insurance, at the expense of the company, for the benefit of any relevant director in respect of any relevant loss.

(2) In this article:

a) a "relevant director" means any director or former director of the company or an associated company,

b) a "relevant loss" means any loss or liability which has been or may be incurred by a relevant director in connection with that director's duties or powers in relation to the company, any associated company or any pension fund or employees' share scheme of the company or an associated company, and

c) companies are associated if one is a subsidiary of the other or both are subsidiaries of the same body corporate.

APPENDIX F
Model articles for private companies limited by guarantee

INDEX TO THE ARTICLES

PART 1: INTERPRETATION AND LIMITATION OF LIABILITY

PART 2: DIRECTORS
DIRECTORS' POWERS AND RESPONSIBILITIES

DECISION-MAKING BY DIRECTORS

APPOINTMENT OF DIRECTORS

PART 3: MEMBERS
BECOMING AND CEASING TO BE A MEMBER

ORGANISATION OF GENERAL MEETINGS

VOTING AT GENERAL MEETINGS

PART 4: ADMINISTRATIVE ARRANGEMENTS

DIRECTORS' INDEMNITY AND INSURANCE

PART 1: DEFINITIONS AND INTERPRETATION

Defined terms

1. In the articles, unless the context requires otherwise:

   - "articles" means the company's articles of association;
   - "bankruptcy" includes individual insolvency proceedings in a jurisdiction other than England and Wales or Northern Ireland which have an effect similar to that of bankruptcy;
   - "chairman" has the meaning given in article 12;
   - "chairman of the meeting" has the meaning given in article 25;

- "Companies Acts" means the Companies Acts (as defined in section 2 of the Companies Act 2006), in so far as they apply to the company;
- "director" means a director of the company, and includes any person occupying the position of director, by whatever name called;
- "document" includes, unless otherwise specified, any document sent or supplied in electronic form;
- "electronic form" has the meaning given in section 1168 of the Companies Act 2006;
- "member" has the meaning given in section 112 of the Companies Act 2006;
- "ordinary resolution" has the meaning given in section 282 of the Companies Act 2006;
- "participate", in relation to a directors' meeting, has the meaning given in article 10;
- "proxy notice" has the meaning given in article 31;
- "special resolution" has the meaning given in section 283 of the Companies Act 2006;
- "subsidiary" has the meaning given in section 1159 of the Companies Act 2006; and
- "writing" means the representation or reproduction of words, symbols or other information in a visible form by any method or combination of methods, whether sent or supplied in electronic form or otherwise.

Unless the context otherwise requires, other words or expressions contained in these articles bear the same meaning as in the Companies Act 2006 as in force on the date when these articles become binding on the company.

Liability of members

2. The liability of each member is limited to £1, being the amount that each member undertakes to contribute to the assets of the company in the event of its being wound up while he is a member or within one year after he ceases to be a member, for:

- payment of the company's debts and liabilities contracted before he ceases to be a member,
- payment of the costs, charges and expenses of winding up, and
- adjustment of the rights of the contributories among themselves.

PART 2: DIRECTORS
DIRECTORS' POWERS AND RESPONSIBILITIES

Directors' general authority

3. Subject to the articles, the directors are responsible for the management of the company's business, for which purpose they may exercise all the powers of the company.

Members' reserve power

4. (1) The members may, by special resolution, direct the directors to take, or refrain from taking, specified action.

(2) No such special resolution invalidates anything which the directors have done before the passing of the resolution.

Directors may delegate

5. (1) Subject to the articles, the directors may delegate any of the powers which are conferred on them under the articles:

a) to such person or committee;

b) by such means (including by power of attorney);

c) to such an extent;

d) in relation to such matters or territories; and

e) on such terms and conditions;

as they think fit.

(2) If the directors so specify, any such delegation may authorise further delegation of the directors' powers by any person to whom they are delegated.

(3) The directors may revoke any delegation in whole or part, or alter its terms and conditions.

Committees

6. (1) Committees to which the directors delegate any of their powers must follow procedures which are based as far as they are applicable on those provisions of the articles which govern the taking of decisions by directors.

(2) The directors may make rules of procedure for all or any committees, which prevail over rules derived from the articles if they are not consistent with them.

DECISION-MAKING BY DIRECTORS

Directors to take decisions collectively

7. (1) The general rule about decision-making by directors is that any decision of the directors must be either a majority decision at a meeting or a decision taken in accordance with article 8.

(2) If:

a) the company only has one director, and

b) no provision of the articles requires it to have more than one director,

the general rule does not apply, and the director may take decisions without regard to any of the provisions of the articles relating to directors' decision-making.

Unanimous decisions

8. (1) A decision of the directors is taken in accordance with this article when all eligible directors indicate to each other by any means that they share a common view on a matter.

(2) Such a decision may take the form of a resolution in writing, copies of which have been signed by each eligible director or to which each eligible director has otherwise indicated agreement in writing.

(3) References in this article to eligible directors are to directors who would have been entitled to vote on the matter had it been proposed as a resolution at a directors' meeting.

(4) A decision may not be taken in accordance with this article if the eligible directors would not have formed a quorum at such a meeting.

Calling a directors' meeting

9. (1) Any director may call a directors' meeting by giving notice of the meeting to the directors or by authorising the company secretary (if any) to give such notice.

(2) Notice of any directors' meeting must indicate:

a) its proposed date and time;

b) where it is to take place; and

c) if it is anticipated that directors participating in the meeting will not be in the same place, how it is proposed that they should communicate with each other during the meeting.

(3) Notice of a directors' meeting must be given to each director, but need not be in writing.

(4) Notice of a directors' meeting need not be given to directors who waive their entitlement to notice of that meeting, by giving notice to that effect to the company not more than 7 days after the date on which the meeting is held. Where such notice is given after the meeting has been held, that does not affect the validity of the meeting, or of any business conducted at it.

Participation in directors' meetings

10. (1) Subject to the articles, directors participate in a directors' meeting, or part of a directors' meeting, when:

a) the meeting has been called and takes place in accordance with the articles, and

b) they can each communicate to the others any information or opinions they have on any particular item of the business of the meeting.

(2) In determining whether directors are participating in a directors' meeting, it is irrelevant where any director is or how they communicate with each other.

(3) If all the directors participating in a meeting are not in the same place, they may decide that the meeting is to be treated as taking place wherever any of them is.

Quorum for directors' meetings

11. (1) At a directors' meeting, unless a quorum is participating, no proposal is to be voted on, except a proposal to call another meeting.

(2) The quorum for directors' meetings may be fixed from time to time by a decision of the directors, but it must never be less than two, and unless otherwise fixed it is two.

(3) If the total number of directors for the time being is less than the quorum required, the directors must not take any decision other than a decision:

a) to appoint further directors, or

b) to call a general meeting so as to enable the members to appoint further directors.

Chairing of directors' meetings

12. (1) The directors may appoint a director to chair their meetings.

(2) The person so appointed for the time being is known as the chairman.

(3) The directors may terminate the chairman's appointment at any time.

(4) If the chairman is not participating in a directors' meeting within ten minutes of the time at which it was to start, the participating directors must appoint one of themselves to chair it.

Casting vote

13. (1) If the numbers of votes for and against a proposal are equal, the chairman or other director chairing the meeting has a casting vote.

(2) But this does not apply if, in accordance with the articles, the chairman or other director is not to be counted as participating in the decision-making process for quorum or voting purposes.

Conflicts of interest

14. (1) If a proposed decision of the directors is concerned with an actual or proposed transaction or arrangement with the company in which a director is interested, that director is not to be counted as participating in the decision-making process for quorum or voting purposes.

(2) But if paragraph (3) applies, a director who is interested in an actual or proposed transaction or arrangement with the company is to be counted as participating in the decision-making process for quorum and voting purposes.

(3) This paragraph applies when:

a) the company by ordinary resolution disapplies the provision of the articles which would otherwise prevent a director from being counted as participating in the decision-making process;

b) the director's interest cannot reasonably be regarded as likely to give rise to a conflict of interest; or

c) the director's conflict of interest arises from a permitted cause.

(4) For the purposes of this article, the following are permitted causes:

a) a guarantee given, or to be given, by or to a director in respect of an obligation incurred by or on behalf of the company or any of its subsidiaries;

b) subscription, or an agreement to subscribe, for securities of the company or any of its subsidiaries, or to underwrite, sub-underwrite, or guarantee subscription for any such securities; and

c) arrangements pursuant to which benefits are made available to employees and directors or former employees and directors of the company or any of its subsidiaries which do not provide special benefits for directors or former directors.

(5) For the purposes of this article, references to proposed decisions and decision-making processes include any directors' meeting or part of a directors' meeting.

(6) Subject to paragraph (7), if a question arises at a meeting of directors or of a committee of directors as to the right of a director to participate in the meeting (or part of the meeting) for voting or quorum purposes, the question may, before the conclusion of the meeting, be referred to the chairman whose ruling in relation to any director other than the chairman is to be final and conclusive.

(7) If any question as to the right to participate in the meeting (or part of the meeting) should arise in respect of the chairman, the question is to be decided by a decision of the directors at that meeting, for which purpose the chairman of the meeting is not to be counted as participating in the meeting (or that part of the meeting) for voting or quorum purposes.

Records of decisions to be kept

15. The directors must ensure that the company keeps a record, in writing, for at least 10 years from the date of the decision recorded, of every unanimous or majority decision taken by the directors.

Directors' discretion to make further rules

16. Subject to the articles, the directors may make any rule which they think fit about how they take decisions, and about how such rules are to be recorded or communicated to directors.

APPOINTMENT OF DIRECTORS

Methods of appointing directors

17. (1) Any person who is willing to act as a director, and is permitted by law to do so, may be appointed to be a director:

a) by ordinary resolution, or

b) by a decision of the directors.

(2) In any case where, as a result of death, the company has no members and no directors, the personal representatives of the last member to have died have the right, by notice in writing, to appoint a person to be a director.

(3) For the purposes of paragraph (2), where 2 or more members die in circumstances rendering it uncertain who was the last to die, a younger member is deemed to have survived an older member.

Termination of director's appointment

18. A person ceases to be a director as soon as:

a) that person ceases to be a director by virtue of any provision of the Companies Act 2006 or is prohibited from being a director by law;

b) a bankruptcy order is made against that person;

c) a composition is made with that person's creditors generally in satisfaction of that person's debts;

d) a registered medical practitioner who is treating that person gives a written opinion to the company stating that that person has become physically or mentally incapable of acting as a director and may remain so for more than three months;

e) by reason of that person's mental health, a court makes an order which wholly or partly prevents that person from personally exercising any powers or rights which that person would otherwise have;

f) notification is received by the company from the director that the director is resigning from office, and such resignation or retirement has taken effect in accordance with its terms.

Directors' remuneration

19. (1) Directors may undertake any services for the company that the directors decide.

(2) Directors are entitled to such remuneration as the directors determine:

a) for their services to the company as directors, and

b) for any other service which they undertake for the company.

(3) Subject to the articles, a director's remuneration may:

a) take any form, and

b) include any arrangements in connection with the payment of a pension, allowance or gratuity, or any death, sickness or disability benefits, to or in respect of that director.

(4) Unless the directors decide otherwise, directors' remuneration accrues from day to day.

(5) Unless the directors decide otherwise, directors are not accountable to the company for any remuneration which they receive as directors or other officers or employees of the company's subsidiaries or of any other body corporate in which the company is interested.

Directors' expenses

20. The company may pay any reasonable expenses which the directors properly incur in connection with their attendance at:

    a) meetings of directors or committees of directors,

    b) general meetings, or

    c) separate meetings of the holders of debentures of the company,

    or otherwise in connection with the exercise of their powers and the discharge of their responsibilities in relation to the company.

PART 3: MEMBERS
BECOMING AND CEASING TO BE A MEMBER

Applications for membership

21. No person shall become a member of the company unless:

    a) that person has completed an application for membership in a form approved by the directors, and

    b) the directors have approved the application.

Termination of membership

22. (1) A member may withdraw from membership of the company by giving 7 days' notice to the company in writing.

    (2) Membership is not transferable.

    (3) A person's membership terminates when that person dies or ceases to exist.

ORGANISATION OF GENERAL MEETINGS

Attendance and speaking at general meetings

23. (1) A person is able to exercise the right to speak at a general meeting when that person is in a position to communicate to all those attending the meeting, during the meeting, any information or opinions which that person has on the business of the meeting.

    (2) A person is able to exercise the right to vote at a general meeting when:

    a) that person is able to vote, during the meeting, on resolutions put to the vote at the meeting, and

    b) that person's vote can be taken into account in determining whether or not such resolutions are passed at the same time as the votes of all the other persons attending the meeting.

    (3) The directors may make whatever arrangements they consider appropriate to enable those attending a general meeting to exercise their rights to speak or vote at it.

    (4) In determining attendance at a general meeting, it is immaterial whether any two or more members attending it are in the same place as each other.

    (5) Two or more persons who are not in the same place as each other attend a general meeting if their circumstances are such that if they have (or were to have) rights to speak and vote at that meeting, they are (or would be) able to exercise them.

Quorum for general meetings

24. No business other than the appointment of the chairman of the meeting is to be transacted at a general meeting if the persons attending it do not constitute a quorum.

Chairing general meetings

25. (1) If the directors have appointed a chairman, the chairman shall chair general meetings if present and willing to do so.

(2) If the directors have not appointed a chairman, or if the chairman is unwilling to chair the meeting or is not present within ten minutes of the time at which a meeting was due to start:

a) the directors present, or

b) (if no directors are present), the meeting,

must appoint a director or member to chair the meeting, and the appointment of the chairman of the meeting must be the first business of the meeting.

(3) The person chairing a meeting in accordance with this article is referred to as "the chairman of the meeting".

Attendance and speaking by directors and non-members

26. (1) Directors may attend and speak at general meetings, whether or not they are members.

(2) The chairman of the meeting may permit other persons who are not members of the company to attend and speak at a general meeting.

Adjournment

27. (1) If the persons attending a general meeting within half an hour of the time at which the meeting was due to start do not constitute a quorum, or if during a meeting a quorum ceases to be present, the chairman of the meeting must adjourn it.

(2) The chairman of the meeting may adjourn a general meeting at which a quorum is present if:

a) the meeting consents to an adjournment, or

b) it appears to the chairman of the meeting that an adjournment is necessary to protect the safety of any person attending the meeting or ensure that the business of the meeting is conducted in an orderly manner.

(3) The chairman of the meeting must adjourn a general meeting if directed to do so by the meeting.

(4) When adjourning a general meeting, the chairman of the meeting must:

a) either specify the time and place to which it is adjourned or state that it is to continue at a time and place to be fixed by the directors, and

b) have regard to any directions as to the time and place of any adjournment which have been given by the meeting.

(5) If the continuation of an adjourned meeting is to take place more than 14 days after it was adjourned, the company must give at least 7 clear days' notice of it (that is, excluding the day of the adjourned meeting and the day on which the notice is given):

a) to the same persons to whom notice of the company's general meetings is required to be given, and

b) containing the same information which such notice is required to contain.

(6) No business may be transacted at an adjourned general meeting which could not properly have been transacted at the meeting if the adjournment had not taken place.

VOTING AT GENERAL MEETINGS

Voting: general

28. A resolution put to the vote of a general meeting must be decided on a show of hands unless a poll is duly demanded in accordance with the articles.

Errors and disputes

29. (1) No objection may be raised to the qualification of any person voting at a general meeting except at the meeting or adjourned meeting at which the vote objected to is tendered, and every vote not disallowed at the meeting is valid.

(2) Any such objection must be referred to the chairman of the meeting whose decision is final.

Poll votes

30. (1) A poll on a resolution may be demanded:

a) in advance of the general meeting where it is to be put to the vote, or

b) at a general meeting, either before a show of hands on that resolution or immediately after the result of a show of hands on that resolution is declared.

(2) A poll may be demanded by:

a) the chairman of the meeting;

b) the directors;

c) two or more persons having the right to vote on the resolution; or

d) a person or persons representing not less than one tenth of the total voting rights of all the members having the right to vote on the resolution.

(3) A demand for a poll may be withdrawn if:

a) the poll has not yet been taken, and

b) the chairman of the meeting consents to the withdrawal.

(4) Polls must be taken immediately and in such manner as the chairman of the meeting directs.

Content of proxy notices

31. (1) Proxies may only validly be appointed by a notice in writing (a "proxy notice") which:

a) states the name and address of the member appointing the proxy;

b) identifies the person appointed to be that member's proxy and the general meeting in relation to which that person is appointed;

c) is signed by or on behalf of the member appointing the proxy, or is authenticated in such manner as the directors may determine; and

d) is delivered to the company in accordance with the articles and any instructions contained in the notice of the general meeting to which they relate.

(2) The company may require proxy notices to be delivered in a particular form, and may specify different forms for different purposes.

(3) Proxy notices may specify how the proxy appointed under them is to vote (or that the proxy is to abstain from voting) on one or more resolutions.

(4) Unless a proxy notice indicates otherwise, it must be treated as:

a) allowing the person appointed under it as a proxy discretion as to how to vote on any ancillary or procedural resolutions put to the meeting, and

b) appointing that person as a proxy in relation to any adjournment of the general meeting to which it relates as well as the meeting itself.

Delivery of proxy notices

32. (1) A person who is entitled to attend, speak or vote (either on a show of hands or on a poll) at a general meeting remains so entitled in respect of that meeting or any adjournment of it, even though a valid proxy notice has been delivered to the company by or on behalf of that person.

(2) An appointment under a proxy notice may be revoked by delivering to the company a notice given by or on behalf of the person by whom or on whose behalf the proxy notice was given.

(3) A notice revoking a proxy appointment only takes effect if it is delivered before the start of the meeting or adjourned meeting to which it relates.

(4) If a proxy notice is not executed by the person appointing the proxy, it must be accompanied by written evidence of the authority of the person who executed it to execute it on the appointor's behalf.

Amendments to resolutions

33. (1) An ordinary resolution to be proposed at a general meeting may be amended by ordinary resolution if:

a) notice of the proposed amendment is given to the company in writing by a person entitled to vote at the general meeting at which it is to be proposed not less than 48 hours before the meeting is to take place (or such later time as the chairman of the meeting may determine), and

b) the proposed amendment does not, in the reasonable opinion of the chairman of the meeting, materially alter the scope of the resolution.

(2) A special resolution to be proposed at a general meeting may be amended by ordinary resolution, if:

a) the chairman of the meeting proposes the amendment at the general meeting at which the resolution is to be proposed, and

b) the amendment does not go beyond what is necessary to correct a grammatical or other non-substantive error in the resolution.

(3) If the chairman of the meeting, acting in good faith, wrongly decides that an amendment to a resolution is out of order, the chairman's error does not invalidate the vote on that resolution.

PART 4; ADMINISTRATIVE ARRANGEMENTS

Means of communication to be used

34. (1) Subject to the articles, anything sent or supplied by or to the company under the articles may be sent or supplied in any way in which the Companies Act 2006 provides for documents or information which are authorised or required by any provision of that Act to be sent or supplied by or to the company.

(2) Subject to the articles, any notice or document to be sent or supplied to a director in connection with the taking of decisions by directors may also be sent or supplied by the means by which that director has asked to be sent or supplied with such notices or documents for the time being.

(3) A director may agree with the company that notices or documents sent to that director in a particular way are to be deemed to have been received within a specified time of their being sent, and for the specified time to be less than 48 hours.

Company seals

35. (1) Any common seal may only be used by the authority of the directors.

(2) The directors may decide by what means and in what form any common seal is to be used.

(3) Unless otherwise decided by the directors, if the company has a common seal and it is affixed to a document, the document must also be signed by at least one authorised person in the presence of a witness who attests the signature.

(4) For the purposes of this article, an authorised person is:

a) any director of the company;

b) the company secretary (if any); or

c) any person authorised by the directors for the purpose of signing documents to which the common seal is applied.

No right to inspect accounts and other records

36. Except as provided by law or authorised by the directors or an ordinary resolution of the company, no person is entitled to inspect any of the company's accounting or other records or documents merely by virtue of being a member.

Provision for employees on cessation of business

37. The directors may decide to make provision for the benefit of persons employed or formerly employed by the company or any of its subsidiaries (other than a director or former director or shadow director) in connection with the cessation or transfer to any person of the whole or part of the undertaking of the company or that subsidiary.

DIRECTORS' INDEMNITY AND INSURANCE

Indemnity

38. (1) Subject to paragraph (2), a relevant director of the company or an associated company may be indemnified out of the company's assets against:

a) any liability incurred by that director in connection with any negligence, default, breach of duty or breach of trust in relation to the company or an associated company,

b) any liability incurred by that director in connection with the activities of the company or an associated company in its capacity as a trustee of an occupational pension scheme (as defined in section 235(6) of the Companies Act 2006),

c) any other liability incurred by that director as an officer of the company or an associated company.

(2) This article does not authorise any indemnity which would be prohibited or rendered void by any provision of the Companies Acts or by any other provision of law.

(3) In this article:

a) companies are associated if one is a subsidiary of the other or both are subsidiaries of the same body corporate, and

b) a "relevant director" means any director or former director of the company or an associated company.

Insurance

39. (1) The directors may decide to purchase and maintain insurance, at the expense of the company, for the benefit of any relevant officer in respect of any relevant loss.

(2) In this article:

a) a "relevant director" means any director or former director of the company or an associated company.

b) a "relevant loss" means any loss or liability which has been or may be incurred by a relevant director in connection with that director's duties or powers in relation to the company, any associated company or any pension fund or employees' share scheme of the company or associated company, and

c) companies are associated if one is a subsidiary of the other or both are subsidiaries of the same body corporate.

APPENDIX G
Model articles for public companies

INDEX TO THE ARTICLES

PART 1: INTERPRETATION AND LIMITATION OF LIABILITY

PART 2: DIRECTORS
DIRECTORS' POWERS AND RESPONSIBILITIES

DECISION-MAKING BY DIRECTORS

APPOINTMENT OF DIRECTORS

ALTERNATE DIRECTORS

25. Appointment and removal of alternates

26. Rights and responsibilities of alternate directors

27. Termination of alternate directorship

PART 3: DECISION-MAKING BY MEMBERS ORGANISATION OF GENERAL MEETINGS

28. Members can call general meeting if not enough directors

29. Attendance and speaking at general meetings

30. Quorum for general meetings

31. Chairing general meetings

32. Attendance and speaking by directors and non-members

33. Adjournment

VOTING AT GENERAL MEETINGS

34. Voting: general

35. Errors and disputes

36. Demanding a poll

37. Procedure on a poll

38. Content of proxy notices

39. Delivery of proxy notices

40. Amendments to resolutions

RESTRICTIONS ON MEMBERS' RIGHTS

41. No voting of shares on which money owed to company

APPLICATION OF RULES TO CLASS MEETINGS

42. Class meetings

PART 4: SHARES AND DISTRIBUTIONS ISSUE OF SHARES

43. Powers to issue different classes of share

44. Payment of commissions on subscription for shares

INTERESTS IN SHARES

45. Company not bound by less than absolute interests

SHARE CERTIFICATES

46. Certificates to be issued except in certain cases

47. Contents and execution of share certificates

CAPITALISATION OF PROFITS

PART 5: MISCELLANEOUS PROVISIONS COMMUNICATIONS

ADMINISTRATIVE ARRANGEMENTS

DIRECTORS' INDEMNITY AND INSURANCE

PART 1: INTERPRETATION AND LIMITATION OF LIABILITY

Defined terms

1. In the articles, unless the context requires otherwise:

   - "alternate" or "alternate director" has the meaning given in article 25;
   - "appointor" has the meaning given in article 25;
   - "articles" means the company's articles of association;
   - "bankruptcy" includes individual insolvency proceedings in a jurisdiction other than England and Wales or Northern Ireland which have an effect similar to that of bankruptcy;
   - "call" has the meaning given in article 54;
   - "call notice" has the meaning given in article 54;
   - "certificate" means a paper certificate (other than a share warrant) evidencing a person's title to specified shares or other securities;
   - "certificated" in relation to a share, means that it is not an uncertificated share or a share in respect of which a share warrant has been issued and is current;
   - "chairman" has the meaning given in article 12;
   - "chairman of the meeting" has the meaning given in article 31;
   - "Companies Acts" means the Companies Acts (as defined in section 2 of the Companies Act 2006), in so far as they apply to the company;
   - "company's lien" has the meaning given in article 52;

- "director" means a director of the company, and includes any person occupying the position of director, by whatever name called;
- "distribution recipient" has the meaning given in article 72;
- "document" includes, unless otherwise specified, any document sent or supplied in electronic form;
- "electronic form" has the meaning given in section 1168 of the Companies Act 2006;
- "fully paid" in relation to a share, means that the nominal value and any premium to be paid to the company in respect of that share have been paid to the company;
- "hard copy form" has the meaning given in section 1168 of the Companies Act 2006;
- "holder" in relation to shares means the person whose name is entered in the register of members as the holder of the shares, or, in the case of a share in respect of which a share warrant has been issued (and not cancelled), the person in possession of that warrant;
- "instrument" means a document in hard copy form;
- "lien enforcement notice" has the meaning given in article 53;
- "member" has the meaning given in section 112 of the Companies Act 2006;
- "ordinary resolution" has the meaning given in section 282 of the Companies Act 2006;
- "paid" means paid or credited as paid;
- "participate", in relation to a directors' meeting, has the meaning given in article 9;
- "partly paid" in relation to a share means that part of that share's nominal value or any premium at which it was issued has not been paid to the company;
- "proxy notice" has the meaning given in article 38;
- "securities seal" has the meaning given in article 47;
- "shares" means shares in the company;
- "special resolution" has the meaning given in section 283 of the Companies Act 2006;
- "subsidiary" has the meaning given in section 1159 of the Companies Act 2006;
- "transmittee" means a person entitled to a share by reason of the death or bankruptcy of a shareholder or otherwise by operation of law;
- "uncertificated" in relation to a share means that, by virtue of legislation (other than section 778 of the Companies Act 2006) permitting title to shares to be evidenced and transferred without a certificate, title to that share is evidenced and may be transferred without a certificate; and
- "writing" means the representation or reproduction of words, symbols or other information in a visible form by any method or combination of methods, whether sent or supplied in electronic form or otherwise.

Unless the context otherwise requires, other words or expressions contained in these articles bear the same meaning as in the Companies Act 2006 as in force on the date when these articles become binding on the company.

Liability of members

2. The liability of the members is limited to the amount, if any, unpaid on the shares held by them.

PART 2: DIRECTORS
DIRECTORS' POWERS AND RESPONSIBILITIES

Directors' general authority

3. Subject to the articles, the directors are responsible for the management of the company's business, for which purpose they may exercise all the powers of the company.

Members' reserve power

4. (1) The members may, by special resolution, direct the directors to take, or refrain from taking, specified action.

   (2) No such special resolution invalidates anything which the directors have done before the passing of the resolution.

   Directors may delegate

5. (1) Subject to the articles, the directors may delegate any of the powers which are conferred on them under the articles:

   a) to such person or committee;

   b) by such means (including by power of attorney);

   c) to such an extent;

   d) in relation to such matters or territories; and

   e) on such terms and conditions;

   as they think fit.

   (2) If the directors so specify, any such delegation may authorise further delegation of the directors' powers by any person to whom they are delegated.

   (3) The directors may revoke any delegation in whole or part, or alter its terms and conditions.

Committees

6. (1) Committees to which the directors delegate any of their powers must follow procedures which are based as far as they are applicable on those provisions of the articles which govern the taking of decisions by directors.

   (2) The directors may make rules of procedure for all or any committees, which prevail over rules derived from the articles if they are not consistent with them.

DECISION-MAKING BY DIRECTORS

Directors to take decisions collectively

7. Decisions of the directors may be taken:

   a) at a directors' meeting, or

   b) in the form of a directors' written resolution.

Calling a directors' meeting

8. (1) Any director may call a directors' meeting.

(2) The company secretary must call a directors' meeting if a director so requests.

(3) A directors' meeting is called by giving notice of the meeting to the directors.

(4) Notice of any directors' meeting must indicate:

a) its proposed date and time;

b) where it is to take place; and

c) if it is anticipated that directors participating in the meeting will not be in the same place,

how it is proposed that they should communicate with each other during the meeting.

(5) Notice of a directors' meeting must be given to each director, but need not be in writing.

(6) Notice of a directors' meeting need not be given to directors who waive their entitlement to notice of that meeting, by giving notice to that effect to the company not more than 7 days after the date on which the meeting is held. Where such notice is given after the meeting has been held, that does not affect the validity of the meeting, or of any business conducted at it.

Participation in directors' meetings

9. (1) Subject to the articles, directors participate in a directors' meeting, or part of a directors' meeting, when:

a) the meeting has been called and takes place in accordance with the articles, and

b) they can each communicate to the others any information or opinions they have on any particular item of the business of the meeting.

(2) In determining whether directors are participating in a directors' meeting, it is irrelevant where any director is or how they communicate with each other.

(3) If all the directors participating in a meeting are not in the same place, they may decide that the meeting is to be treated as taking place wherever any of them is.

Quorum for directors' meetings

10. (1) At a directors' meeting, unless a quorum is participating, no proposal is to be voted on, except a proposal to call another meeting.

(2) The quorum for directors' meetings may be fixed from time to time by a decision of the directors, but it must never be less than two, and unless otherwise fixed it is two.

Meetings where total number of directors less than quorum

11. (1) This article applies where the total number of directors for the time being is less than the quorum for directors' meetings.

(2) If there is only one director, that director may appoint sufficient directors to make up a quorum or call a general meeting to do so.

(3) If there is more than one director:

a) a directors' meeting may take place, if it is called in accordance with the articles and at least two directors participate in it, with a view to appointing sufficient directors to make up a quorum or calling a general meeting to do so, and

b) if a directors' meeting is called but only one director attends at the appointed date and time to participate in it, that director may appoint sufficient directors to make up a quorum or call a general meeting to do so.

Chairing directors' meetings

12. (1) The directors may appoint a director to chair their meetings.

(2) The person so appointed for the time being is known as the chairman.

(3) The directors may appoint other directors as deputy or assistant chairmen to chair directors' meetings in the chairman's absence.

(4) The directors may terminate the appointment of the chairman, deputy or assistant chairman at any time.

(5) If neither the chairman nor any director appointed generally to chair directors' meetings in the chairman's absence is participating in a meeting within ten minutes of the time at which it was to start, the participating directors must appoint one of themselves to chair it.

Voting at directors' meetings: general rules

13. (1) Subject to the articles, a decision is taken at a directors' meeting by a majority of the votes of the participating directors.

(2) Subject to the articles, each director participating in a directors' meeting has one vote.

(3) Subject to the articles, if a director has an interest in an actual or proposed transaction or arrangement with the company:

a) that director and that director's alternate may not vote on any proposal relating to it, but

b) this does not preclude the alternate from voting in relation to that transaction or arrangement on behalf of another appointor who does not have such an interest.

Chairman's casting vote at directors' meetings

14. (1) If the numbers of votes for and against a proposal are equal, the chairman or other director chairing the meeting has a casting vote.

(2) But this does not apply if, in accordance with the articles, the chairman or other director is not to be counted as participating in the decision-making process for quorum or voting purposes.

Alternates voting at directors' meetings

15. A director who is also an alternate director has an additional vote on behalf of each appointor who is:

a) not participating in a directors' meeting, and

b) would have been entitled to vote if they were participating in it.

Conflicts of interest

16. (1) If a directors' meeting, or part of a directors' meeting, is concerned with an actual or proposed transaction or arrangement with the company in which a director is interested, that director is not to be counted as participating in that meeting, or part of a meeting, for quorum or voting purposes.

(2) But if paragraph (3) applies, a director who is interested in an actual or proposed transaction or arrangement with the company is to be counted as participating in a decision at a directors' meeting, or part of a directors' meeting, relating to it for quorum and voting purposes.

(3) This paragraph applies when:

a) the company by ordinary resolution disapplies the provision of the articles which would otherwise prevent a director from being counted as participating in, or voting at, a directors' meeting;

(b) the director's interest cannot reasonably be regarded as likely to give rise to a conflict of interest; or

(c) the director's conflict of interest arises from a permitted cause.

(4) For the purposes of this article, the following are permitted causes:

a) a guarantee given, or to be given, by or to a director in respect of an obligation incurred by or on behalf of the company or any of its subsidiaries;

b) subscription, or an agreement to subscribe, for shares or other securities of the company or any of its subsidiaries, or to underwrite, sub-underwrite, or guarantee subscription for

any such shares or securities; and

c) arrangements pursuant to which benefits are made available to employees and directors or former employees and directors of the company or any of its subsidiaries which do not provide special benefits for directors or former directors.

(5) Subject to paragraph (6), if a question arises at a meeting of directors or of a committee of directors as to the right of a director to participate in the meeting (or part of the meeting) for voting or quorum purposes, the question may, before the conclusion of the meeting, be referred to the chairman whose ruling in relation to any director other than the chairman is to be final and conclusive.

(6) If any question as to the right to participate in the meeting (or part of the meeting) should arise in respect of the chairman, the question is to be decided by a decision of the directors at that meeting, for which purpose the chairman is not to be counted as participating in the meeting (or that part of the meeting) for voting or quorum purposes.

Proposing directors' written resolutions

17. (1) Any director may propose a directors' written resolution.

(2) The company secretary must propose a directors' written resolution if a director so requests.

(3) A directors' written resolution is proposed by giving notice of the proposed resolution to the directors.

(4) Notice of a proposed directors' written resolution must indicate:

a) the proposed resolution, and

b) the time by which it is proposed that the directors should adopt it.

(5) Notice of a proposed directors' written resolution must be given in writing to each director.

(6) Any decision which a person giving notice of a proposed directors' written resolution takes regarding the process of adopting that resolution must be taken reasonably in good faith.

Adoption of directors' written resolutions

18. (1) A proposed directors' written resolution is adopted when all the directors who would have been entitled to vote on the resolution at a directors' meeting have signed one or more copies of it, provided that those directors would have formed a quorum at such a meeting.

(2) It is immaterial whether any director signs the resolution before or after the time by which the notice proposed that it should be adopted.

(3) Once a directors' written resolution has been adopted, it must be treated as if it had been a decision taken at a directors' meeting in accordance with the articles.

(4) The company secretary must ensure that the company keeps a record, in writing, of all directors' written resolutions for at least ten years from the date of their adoption.

Directors' discretion to make further rules

19. Subject to the articles, the directors may make any rule which they think fit about how they take decisions, and about how such rules are to be recorded or communicated to directors.

APPOINTMENT OF DIRECTORS

Methods of appointing directors

20. Any person who is willing to act as a director, and is permitted by law to do so, may be appointed to be a director:

a) by ordinary resolution, or

b) by a decision of the directors.

Retirement of directors by rotation

21. (1) At the first annual general meeting all the directors must retire from office.

(2) At every subsequent annual general meeting any directors:

a) who have been appointed by the directors since the last annual general meeting, or

b) who were not appointed or reappointed at one of the preceding two annual general meetings,

must retire from office and may offer themselves for reappointment by the members.

Termination of director's appointment

22. A person ceases to be a director as soon as:

a) that person ceases to be a director by virtue of any provision of the Companies Act 2006 or is prohibited from being a director by law;

b) a bankruptcy order is made against that person;

c) a composition is made with that person's creditors generally in satisfaction of that person's debts;

d) a registered medical practitioner who is treating that person gives a written opinion to the company stating that that person has become physically or mentally incapable of acting as a director and may remain so for more than three months;

e) by reason of that person's mental health, a court makes an order which wholly or partly prevents that person from personally exercising any powers or rights which that person would otherwise have;

f) notification is received by the company from the director that the director is resigning from office as director, and such resignation has taken effect in accordance with its terms.

Directors' remuneration

23. (1) Directors may undertake any services for the company that the directors decide.

(2) Directors are entitled to such remuneration as the directors determine:

a) for their services to the company as directors, and

b) for any other service which they undertake for the company.

(3) Subject to the articles, a director's remuneration may:

a) take any form, and

b) include any arrangements in connection with the payment of a pension, allowance or gratuity, or any death, sickness or disability benefits, to or in respect of that director.

(4) Unless the directors decide otherwise, directors' remuneration accrues from day to day.

(5) Unless the directors decide otherwise, directors are not accountable to the company for any remuneration which they receive as directors or other officers or employees of the company's subsidiaries or of any other body corporate in which the company is interested.

Directors' expenses

24. The company may pay any reasonable expenses which the directors properly incur in connection with their attendance at:

a) meetings of directors or committees of directors,

b) general meetings, or

c) separate meetings of the holders of any class of shares or of debentures of the company,

or otherwise in connection with the exercise of their powers and the discharge of their responsibilities in relation to the company.

ALTERNATE DIRECTORS

Appointment and removal of alternates

25. (1) Any director (the "appointor") may appoint as an alternate any other director, or any other person approved by resolution of the directors, to:

a) exercise that director's powers, and

b) carry out that director's responsibilities, in relation to the taking of decisions by the directors in the absence of the alternate's appointor.

(2) Any appointment or removal of an alternate must be effected by notice in writing to the company signed by the appointor, or in any other manner approved by the directors.

(3) The notice must:

a) identify the proposed alternate, and

b) in the case of a notice of appointment, contain a statement signed by the proposed alternate that the proposed alternate is willing to act as the alternate of the director giving the notice.

Rights and responsibilities of alternate directors

26. (1) An alternate director has the same rights, in relation to any directors' meeting or directors' written resolution, as the alternate's appointor.

(2) Except as the articles specify otherwise, alternate directors:

a) are deemed for all purposes to be directors;

b) are liable for their own acts and omissions;

c) are subject to the same restrictions as their appointors; and

d) are not deemed to be agents of or for their appointors.

(3) A person who is an alternate director but not a director:

a) may be counted as participating for the purposes of determining whether a quorum is participating (but only if that person's appointor is not participating), and

b) may sign a written resolution (but only if it is not signed or to be signed by that person's appointor).

No alternate may be counted as more than one director for such purposes.

(4) An alternate director is not entitled to receive any remuneration from the company for serving as an alternate director except such part of the alternate's appointor's remuneration as the appointor may direct by notice in writing made to the company.

Termination of alternate directorship

27. An alternate director's appointment as an alternate terminates:

a) when the alternate's appointor revokes the appointment by notice to the company in writing specifying when it is to terminate;

b) on the occurrence in relation to the alternate of any event which, if it occurred in relation to the alternate's appointor, would result in the termination of the appointor's appointment as a director;

c) on the death of the alternate's appointor; or

d) when the alternate's appointor's appointment as a director terminates, except that an alternate's appointment as an alternate does not terminate when the appointor retires by rotation at a general meeting and is then re-appointed as a director at the same general meeting.

PART 3: DECISION-MAKING BY MEMBERS ORGANISATION OF GENERAL MEETINGS

Members can call general meeting if not enough directors

28. If:

a) the company has fewer than two directors, and

b) the director (if any) is unable or unwilling to appoint sufficient directors to make up a quorum or to call a general meeting to do so, then two or more members may call a general meeting (or instruct the company secretary to do so) for the purpose of appointing one or more directors.

Attendance and speaking at general meetings

29. (1) A person is able to exercise the right to speak at a general meeting when that person is in a position to communicate to all those attending the meeting, during the meeting, any information or opinions which that person has on the business of the meeting.

(2) A person is able to exercise the right to vote at a general meeting when:

a) that person is able to vote, during the meeting, on resolutions put to the vote at the meeting, and

b) that person's vote can be taken into account in determining whether or not such resolutions are passed at the same time as the votes of all the other persons attending the meeting.

(3) The directors may make whatever arrangements they consider appropriate to enable those attending a general meeting to exercise their rights to speak or vote at it.

(4) In determining attendance at a general meeting, it is immaterial whether any two or more members attending it are in the same place as each other.

(5) Two or more persons who are not in the same place as each other attend a general meeting if their circumstances are such that if they have (or were to have) rights to speak and vote at that meeting, they are (or would be) able to exercise them.

Quorum for general meetings

30. No business other than the appointment of the chairman of the meeting is to be transacted at a general meeting if the persons attending it do not constitute a quorum.

Chairing general meetings

31. (1) If the directors have appointed a chairman, the chairman shall chair general meetings if present and willing to do so.

(2) If the directors have not appointed a chairman, or if the chairman is unwilling to chair the meeting or is not present within ten minutes of the time at which a meeting was due to start:

a) the directors present, or

b) (if no directors are present), the meeting,

must appoint a director or member to chair the meeting, and the appointment of the chairman of the meeting must be the first business of the meeting.

(3) The person chairing a meeting in accordance with this article is referred to as "the chairman of the meeting".

Attendance and speaking by directors and non-members

32. (1) Directors may attend and speak at general meetings, whether or not they are members.

(2) The chairman of the meeting may permit other persons who are not:

a) members of the company, or

b) otherwise entitled to exercise the rights of members in relation to general meetings,

to attend and speak at a general meeting.

Adjournment

33. (1) If the persons attending a general meeting within half an hour of the time at which the meeting was due to start do not constitute a quorum, or if during a meeting a quorum ceases to be present, the chairman of the meeting must adjourn it.

(2) The chairman of the meeting may adjourn a general meeting at which a quorum is present if:

a) the meeting consents to an adjournment, or

b) it appears to the chairman of the meeting that an adjournment is necessary to protect the safety of any person attending the meeting or ensure that the business of the meeting is conducted in an orderly manner.

(3) The chairman of the meeting must adjourn a general meeting if directed to do so by the meeting.

(4) When adjourning a general meeting, the chairman of the meeting must:

a) either specify the time and place to which it is adjourned or state that it is to continue at a time and place to be fixed by the directors, and

b) have regard to any directions as to the time and place of any adjournment which have been given by the meeting.

(5) If the continuation of an adjourned meeting is to take place more than 14 days after it was adjourned, the company must give at least 7 clear days' notice of it (that is, excluding the day of the adjourned meeting and the day on which the notice is given):

a) to the same persons to whom notice of the company's general meetings is required to be given, and

b) containing the same information which such notice is required to contain.

(6) No business may be transacted at an adjourned general meeting which could not properly have been transacted at the meeting if the adjournment had not taken place.

VOTING AT GENERAL MEETINGS

Voting: general

34. resolution put to the vote of a general meeting must be decided on a show of hands unless a poll is duly demanded in accordance with the articles.

Errors and disputes

35. (1) No objection may be raised to the qualification of any person voting at a general meeting except at the meeting or adjourned meeting at which the vote objected to is tendered, and every vote not disallowed at the meeting is valid.

(2) Any such objection must be referred to the chairman of the meeting whose decision is final.

Demanding a poll

36. (1) A poll on a resolution may be demanded:

a) in advance of the general meeting where it is to be put to the vote, or

b) at a general meeting, either before a show of hands on that resolution or immediately after the result of a show of hands on that resolution is declared.

(2) A poll may be demanded by:

a) the chairman of the meeting;

b) the directors;

c) two or more persons having the right to vote on the resolution; or

d) a person or persons representing not less than one tenth of the total voting rights of all the members having the right to vote on the resolution.

(3) A demand for a poll may be withdrawn if:

a) the poll has not yet been taken, and

b) the chairman of the meeting consents to the withdrawal.

Procedure on a poll

37. (1) Subject to the articles, polls at general meetings must be taken when, where and in such manner as the chairman of the meeting directs.

(2) The chairman of the meeting may appoint scrutineers (who need not be members) and decide how and when the result of the poll is to be declared.

(3) The result of a poll shall be the decision of the meeting in respect of the resolution on which the poll was demanded.

(4) A poll on:

a) the election of the chairman of the meeting, or

b) a question of adjournment, must be taken immediately.

(5) Other polls must be taken within 30 days of their being demanded.

(6) A demand for a poll does not prevent a general meeting from continuing, except as regards the question on which the poll was demanded.

(7) No notice need be given of a poll not taken immediately if the time and place at which it is to be taken are announced at the meeting at which it is demanded.

(8) In any other case, at least 7 days' notice must be given specifying the time and place at which the poll is to be taken.

Content of proxy notices

38. (1) Proxies may only validly be appointed by a notice in writing (a "proxy notice") which:

a) states the name and address of the member appointing the proxy;

b) identifies the person appointed to be that member's proxy and the general meeting in relation to which that person is appointed;

c) is signed by or on behalf of the member appointing the proxy, or is authenticated in such manner as the directors may determine; and

d) is delivered to the company in accordance with the articles and any instructions contained in the notice of the general meeting to which they relate.

(2) The company may require proxy notices to be delivered in a particular form, and may specify different forms for different purposes.

(3) Proxy notices may specify how the proxy appointed under them is to vote (or that the proxy is to abstain from voting) on one or more resolutions.

(4) Unless a proxy notice indicates otherwise, it must be treated as:

a) allowing the person appointed under it as a proxy discretion as to how to vote on any ancillary or procedural resolutions put to the meeting, and

b) appointing that person as a proxy in relation to any adjournment of the general meeting to which it relates as well as the meeting itself.

Delivery of proxy notices

39. (1) Any notice of a general meeting must specify the address or addresses ("proxy notification address") at which the company or its agents will receive proxy notices relating to that meeting, or any adjournment of it, delivered in hard copy or electronic form.

(2) A person who is entitled to attend, speak or vote (either on a show of hands or on a poll) at a general meeting remains so entitled in respect of that meeting or any adjournment of it, even though a valid proxy notice has been delivered to the company by or on behalf of that person.

(3) Subject to paragraphs (4) and (5), a proxy notice must be delivered to a proxy notification address not less than 48 hours before the general meeting or adjourned meeting to which it relates.

(4) In the case of a poll taken more than 48 hours after it is demanded, the notice must be delivered to a proxy notification address not less than 24 hours before the time appointed for the taking of the poll.

(5) In the case of a poll not taken during the meeting but taken not more than 48 hours after it was demanded, the proxy notice must be delivered:

a) in accordance with paragraph (3), or

b) at the meeting at which the poll was demanded to the chairman, secretary or any director.

(6) An appointment under a proxy notice may be revoked by delivering a notice in writing given by or on behalf of the person by whom or on whose behalf the proxy notice was given to a proxy notification address.

(7) A notice revoking a proxy appointment only takes effect if it is delivered before:

a) the start of the meeting or adjourned meeting to which it relates, or

b) (in the case of a poll not taken on the same day as the meeting or adjourned meeting) the time appointed for taking the poll to which it relates.

(8) If a proxy notice is not signed by the person appointing the proxy, it must be accompanied by written evidence of the authority of the person who executed it to execute it on the appointor's behalf.

Amendments to resolutions

40. (1) An ordinary resolution to be proposed at a general meeting may be amended by ordinary resolution if:

a) notice of the proposed amendment is given to the company secretary in writing by a person entitled to vote at the general meeting at which it is to be proposed not less than 48 hours before the meeting is to take place (or such later time as the chairman of the meeting may determine), and

b) the proposed amendment does not, in the reasonable opinion of the chairman of the meeting, materially alter the scope of the resolution.

(2) A special resolution to be proposed at a general meeting may be amended by ordinary resolution, if:

a) the chairman of the meeting proposes the amendment at the general meeting at which the resolution is to be proposed, and

b) the amendment does not go beyond what is necessary to correct a grammatical or other non-substantive error in the resolution.

(3) If the chairman of the meeting, acting in good faith, wrongly decides that an amendment to a resolution is out of order, the chairman's error does not invalidate the vote on that resolution.

RESTRICTIONS ON MEMBERS' RIGHTS

No voting of shares on which money owed to company

41. No voting rights attached to a share may be exercised at any general meeting, at any adjournment of it, or on any poll called at or in relation to it, unless all amounts payable to the company in respect of that share have been paid.

APPLICATION OF RULES TO CLASS MEETINGS

Class meetings

42. The provisions of the articles relating to general meetings apply, with any necessary modifications, to meetings of the holders of any class of shares.

PART 4: SHARES AND DISTRIBUTIONS
ISSUE OF SHARES

Powers to issue different classes of share

43. (1) Subject to the articles, but without prejudice to the rights attached to any existing share, the company may issue shares with such rights or restrictions as may be determined by ordinary resolution.

(2) The company may issue shares which are to be redeemed, or are liable to be redeemed at the option of the company or the holder, and the directors may determine the terms, conditions and manner of redemption of any such shares.

Payment of commissions on subscription for shares

44. (1) The company may pay any person a commission in consideration for that person:

a) subscribing, or agreeing to subscribe, for shares, or

b) procuring, or agreeing to procure, subscriptions for shares.

(2) Any such commission may be paid:

a) in cash, or in fully paid or partly paid shares or other securities, or partly in one way and partly in the other, and (b) in respect of a conditional or an absolute subscription.

INTERESTS IN SHARES

Company not bound by less than absolute interests

45. Except as required by law, no person is to be recognised by the company as holding any share upon any trust, and except as otherwise required by law or the articles, the company is not in any way to be bound by or recognise any interest in a share other than the holder's absolute ownership of it and all the rights attaching to it.

SHARE CERTIFICATES

Certificates to be issued except in certain cases

46. (1) The company must issue each member with one or more certificates in respect of the shares which that member holds.

(2) This article does not apply to:

a) uncertificated shares;

b) shares in respect of which a share warrant has been issued; or

c) shares in respect of which the Companies Acts permit the company not to issue a certificate.

(3) Except as otherwise specified in the articles, all certificates must be issued free of charge.

(4) No certificate may be issued in respect of shares of more than one class.

(5) If more than one person holds a share, only one certificate may be issued in respect of it.

Contents and execution of share certificates

47. (1) Every certificate must specify:

a) in respect of how many shares, of what class, it is issued;

b) the nominal value of those shares;

c) the amount paid up on them; and

d) any distinguishing numbers assigned to them.

(2) Certificates must:

a) have affixed to them the company's common seal or an official seal which is a facsimile of the company's common seal with the addition on its face of the word "Securities" (a "securities seal"), or

b) be otherwise executed in accordance with the Companies Acts.

Consolidated share certificates

48. (1) When a member's holding of shares of a particular class increases, the company may issue that member with:

a) a single, consolidated certificate in respect of all the shares of a particular class which that member holds, or

b) a separate certificate in respect of only those shares by which that member's holding has increased.

(2) When a member's holding of shares of a particular class is reduced, the company must ensure that the member is issued with one or more certificates in respect of

the number of shares held by the member after that reduction. But the company need not (in the absence of a request from the member) issue any new certificate if:

a) all the shares which the member no longer holds as a result of the reduction, and

b) none of the shares which the member retains following the reduction, were, immediately before the reduction, represented by the same certificate.

(3) A member may request the company, in writing, to replace:

a) the member's separate certificates with a consolidated certificate, or

b) the member's consolidated certificate with two or more separate certificates representing such proportion of the shares as the member may specify.

(4) When the company complies with such a request it may charge such reasonable fee as the directors may decide for doing so.

(5) A consolidated certificate must not be issued unless any certificates which it is to replace have first been returned to the company for cancellation.

Replacement share certificates

49. (1) If a certificate issued in respect of a member's shares is:

a) damaged or defaced, or

b) said to be lost, stolen or destroyed, that member is entitled to be issued with a replacement certificate in respect of the same shares.

(2) A member exercising the right to be issued with such a replacement certificate:

a) may at the same time exercise the right to be issued with a single certificate or separate certificates;

b) must return the certificate which is to be replaced to the company if it is damaged or defaced; and

c) must comply with such conditions as to evidence, indemnity and the payment of a reasonable fee as the directors decide.

SHARES NOT HELD IN CERTIFICATED FORM

Uncertificated shares

50. (1) In this article, "the relevant rules" means:

a) any applicable provision of the Companies Acts about the holding, evidencing of title to, or transfer of shares other than in certificated form, and

b) any applicable legislation, rules or other arrangements made under or by virtue of such provision.

(2) The provisions of this article have effect subject to the relevant rules.

(3) Any provision of the articles which is inconsistent with the relevant rules must be disregarded, to the extent that it is inconsistent, whenever the relevant rules apply.

(4) Any share or class of shares of the company may be issued or held on such terms, or in such a way, that:

a) title to it or them is not, or must not be, evidenced by a certificate, or

b) it or they may or must be transferred wholly or partly without a certificate.

(5) The directors have power to take such steps as they think fit in relation to:

a) the evidencing of and transfer of title to uncertificated shares (including in connection with the issue of such shares);

b) any records relating to the holding of uncertificated shares;

c) the conversion of certificated shares into uncertificated shares; or

d) the conversion of uncertificated shares into certificated shares.

(6) The company may by notice to the holder of a share require that share:

a) if it is uncertificated, to be converted into certificated form, and (b) if it is certificated, to be converted into uncertificated form, to enable it to be dealt with in accordance with the articles.

(7) If:

a) the articles give the directors power to take action, or require other persons to take action, in order to sell, transfer or otherwise dispose of shares, and

b) uncertificated shares are subject to that power, but the power is expressed in terms which assume the use of a certificate or other written instrument, the directors may take such action as is necessary or expedient to achieve the same results when exercising that power in relation to uncertificated shares.

(8) In particular, the directors may take such action as they consider appropriate to achieve the sale, transfer, disposal, forfeiture, re-allotment or surrender of an uncertificated share or otherwise to enforce a lien in respect of it.

(9) Unless the directors otherwise determine, shares which a member holds in uncertificated form must be treated as separate holdings from any shares which that member holds in certificated form.

(10) A class of shares must not be treated as two classes simply because some shares of that class are held in certificated form and others are held in uncertificated form.

Share warrants

51. (1) The directors may issue a share warrant in respect of any fully paid share.

(2) Share warrants must be:

a) issued in such form, and

b) executed in such manner, as the directors decide.

(3) A share represented by a share warrant may be transferred by delivery of the warrant representing it.

(4) The directors may make provision for the payment of dividends in respect of any share represented by a share warrant.

(5) Subject to the articles, the directors may decide the conditions on which any share warrant is issued. In particular, they may:

a) decide the conditions on which new warrants are to be issued in place of warrants which are damaged or defaced, or said to have been lost, stolen or destroyed;

b) decide the conditions on which bearers of warrants are entitled to attend and vote at general meetings;

c) decide the conditions subject to which bearers of warrants may surrender their warrant so as to hold their shares in certificated or uncertificated form instead; and

d) vary the conditions of issue of any warrant from time to time, and the bearer of a warrant is subject to the conditions and procedures in force in relation to it, whether or not they were decided or specified before the warrant was issued.

(6) Subject to the conditions on which the warrants are issued from time to time, bearers of share warrants have the same rights and privileges as they would if their names had been included in the register as holders of the shares represented by their warrants.

(7) The company must not in any way be bound by or recognise any interest in a share represented by a share warrant other than the absolute right of the bearer of that warrant to that warrant.

PARTLY PAID SHARES

Company's lien over partly paid shares

52. (1) The company has a lien ("the company's lien") over every share which is partly paid for any part of:

a) that share's nominal value, and

b) any premium at which it was issued, which has not been paid to the company, and which is payable immediately or at some time in the future, whether or not a call notice has been sent in respect of it.

(2) The company's lien over a share:

a) takes priority over any third party's interest in that share, and

b) extends to any dividend or other money payable by the company in respect of that share and (if the lien is enforced and the share is sold by the company) the proceeds of sale of that share.

(3) The directors may at any time decide that a share which is or would otherwise be subject to the company's lien shall not be subject to it, either wholly or in part.

Enforcement of the company's lien

53. (1) Subject to the provisions of this article, if:

a) a lien enforcement notice has been given in respect of a share, and

b) the person to whom the notice was given has failed to comply with it,

the company may sell that share in such manner as the directors decide.

(2) A lien enforcement notice:

a) may only be given in respect of a share which is subject to the company's lien, in respect of which a sum is payable and the due date for payment of that sum has passed;

b) must specify the share concerned;

c) must require payment of the sum payable within 14 days of the notice;

d) must be addressed either to the holder of the share or to a person entitled to it by reason of the holder's death, bankruptcy or otherwise; and

e) must state the company's intention to sell the share if the notice is not complied with.

(3) Where shares are sold under this article:

a) the directors may authorise any person to execute an instrument of transfer of the shares to the purchaser or a person nominated by the purchaser, and

(b) the transferee is not bound to see to the application of the consideration, and the transferee's title is not affected by any irregularity in or invalidity of the process leading to the sale.

(4) The net proceeds of any such sale (after payment of the costs of sale and any other costs of enforcing the lien) must be applied:

a) first, in payment of so much of the sum for which the lien exists as was payable at the date of the lien enforcement notice,

b) second, to the person entitled to the shares at the date of the sale, but only after the certificate for the shares sold has been surrendered to the company for cancellation or a suitable indemnity has been given for any lost certificates, and subject to a lien equivalent to the company's lien over the shares before the sale for any money payable in respect of the shares after the date of the lien enforcement notice.

(5) A statutory declaration by a director or the company secretary that the declarant is a director or the company secretary and that a share has been sold to satisfy the company's lien on a specified date:

a) is conclusive evidence of the facts stated in it as against all persons claiming to be entitled to the share, and

b) subject to compliance with any other formalities of transfer required by the articles or by law, constitutes a good title to the share.

Call notices

54. (1) Subject to the articles and the terms on which shares are allotted, the directors may send a notice (a "call notice") to a member requiring the member to pay the company a specified sum of money (a "call") which is payable in respect of shares which that member holds at the date when the directors decide to send the call notice.

(2) A call notice:

a) may not require a member to pay a call which exceeds the total sum unpaid on that member's shares (whether as to the share's nominal value or any amount payable to the company by way of premium);

b) must state when and how any call to which it relates it is to be paid; and

c) may permit or require the call to be paid by instalments.

(3) A member must comply with the requirements of a call notice, but no member is obliged to pay any call before 14 days have passed since the notice was sent.

(4) Before the company has received any call due under a call notice the directors may:

a) revoke it wholly or in part, or

b) specify a later time for payment than is specified in the notice, by a further notice in writing to the member in respect of whose shares the call is made.

Liability to pay calls

55. (1) Liability to pay a call is not extinguished or transferred by transferring the shares in respect of which it is required to be paid.

(2) Joint holders of a share are jointly and severally liable to pay all calls in respect of that share.

(3) Subject to the terms on which shares are allotted, the directors may, when issuing shares, provide that call notices sent to the holders of those shares may require them:

a) to pay calls which are not the same, or

b) to pay calls at different times.

When call notice need not be issued

56. (1) A call notice need not be issued in respect of sums which are specified, in the terms on which a share is issued, as being payable to the company in respect of that share (whether in respect of nominal value or premium):

a) on allotment;

b) on the occurrence of a particular event; or

c) on a date fixed by or in accordance with the terms of issue.

(2) But if the due date for payment of such a sum has passed and it has not been paid, the holder of the share concerned is treated in all respects as having failed to comply with a call notice in respect of that sum, and is liable to the same consequences as regards the payment of interest and forfeiture.

Failure to comply with call notice: automatic consequences

57. (1) If a person is liable to pay a call and fails to do so by the call payment date:

a) the directors may issue a notice of intended forfeiture to that person, and

b) until the call is paid, that person must pay the company interest on the call from the call payment date at the relevant rate.

(2) For the purposes of this article:

a) the "call payment date" is the time when the call notice states that a call is payable, unless the directors give a notice specifying a later date, in which case the "call payment date" is that later date;

b) the "relevant rate" is:

i) the rate fixed by the terms on which the share in respect of which the call is due was allotted;

ii) such other rate as was fixed in the call notice which required payment of the call, or has otherwise been determined by the directors; or

iii) if no rate is fixed in either of these ways, 5 per cent per annum.

(3) The relevant rate must not exceed by more than 5 percentage points the base lending rate most recently set by the Monetary Policy Committee of the Bank of England in connection with its responsibilities under Part 2 of the Bank of England Act 1998a).

(4) The directors may waive any obligation to pay interest on a call wholly or in part.

Notice of intended forfeiture

58. A notice of intended forfeiture:

a) may be sent in respect of any share in respect of which a call has not been paid as required by a call notice;

b) must be sent to the holder of that share or to a person entitled to it by reason of the holder's death, bankruptcy or otherwise;

c) must require payment of the call and any accrued interest by a date which is not less than 14 days after the date of the notice;

d) must state how the payment is to be made; and

e) must state that if the notice is not complied with, the shares in respect of which the call is payable will be liable to be forfeited.

Directors' power to forfeit shares

59. If a notice of intended forfeiture is not complied with before the date by which payment of the call is required in the notice of intended forfeiture, the directors may decide that any share in respect of which it was given is forfeited, and the forfeiture is to include all dividends or other moneys payable in respect of the forfeited shares and not paid before the forfeiture.

Effect of forfeiture

60. (1) Subject to the articles, the forfeiture of a share extinguishes:

a) all interests in that share, and all claims and demands against the company in respect of it, and

b) all other rights and liabilities incidental to the share as between the person whose share it was prior to the forfeiture and the company.

(2) Any share which is forfeited in accordance with the articles:

a) is deemed to have been forfeited when the directors decide that it is forfeited;

b) is deemed to be the property of the company; and

c) may be sold, re-allotted or otherwise disposed of as the directors think fit.

(3) If a person's shares have been forfeited:

a) the company must send that person notice that forfeiture has occurred and record it in the register of members;

b) that person ceases to be a member in respect of those shares;

c) that person must surrender the certificate for the shares forfeited to the company for cancellation;

d) that person remains liable to the company for all sums payable by that person under the articles at the date of forfeiture in respect of those shares, including any interest (whether accrued before or after the date of forfeiture); and

e) the directors may waive payment of such sums wholly or in part or enforce payment without any allowance for the value of the shares at the time of forfeiture or for any consideration received on their disposal.

(4) At any time before the company disposes of a forfeited share, the directors may decide to cancel the forfeiture on payment of all calls and interest due in respect of it and on such other terms as they think fit.

Procedure following forfeiture

61. (1) If a forfeited share is to be disposed of by being transferred, the company may receive the consideration for the transfer and the directors may authorise any person to execute the instrument of transfer.

(2) A statutory declaration by a director or the company secretary that the declarant is a director or the company secretary and that a share has been forfeited on a specified date:

a) is conclusive evidence of the facts stated in it as against all persons claiming to be entitled to the share, and

b) subject to compliance with any other formalities of transfer required by the articles or by law, constitutes a good title to the share.

(3) A person to whom a forfeited share is transferred is not bound to see to the application of the consideration (if any) nor is that person's title to the share affected by any irregularity in or invalidity of the process leading to the forfeiture or transfer of the share.

(4) If the company sells a forfeited share, the person who held it prior to its forfeiture is entitled to receive from the company the proceeds of such sale, net of any commission, and excluding any amount which:

a) was, or would have become, payable, and

b) had not, when that share was forfeited, been paid by that person in respect of that share,

but no interest is payable to such a person in respect of such proceeds and the company is not required to account for any money earned on them.

Surrender of shares

62. (1) A member may surrender any share:

a) in respect of which the directors may issue a notice of intended forfeiture;

b) which the directors may forfeit; or

c) which has been forfeited.

(2) The directors may accept the surrender of any such share.

(3) The effect of surrender on a share is the same as the effect of forfeiture on that share.

(4) A share which has been surrendered may be dealt with in the same way as a share which has been forfeited.

TRANSFER AND TRANSMISSION OF SHARES

Transfers of certificated shares

63. (1) Certificated shares may be transferred by means of an instrument of transfer in any usual form or any other form approved by the directors, which is executed by or on behalf of:

a) the transferor, and

b) (if any of the shares is partly paid) the transferee.

(2) No fee may be charged for registering any instrument of transfer or other document relating to or affecting the title to any share.

(3) The company may retain any instrument of transfer which is registered.

(4) The transferor remains the holder of a certificated share until the transferee's name is entered in the register of members as holder of it.

(5) The directors may refuse to register the transfer of a certificated share if:

a) the share is not fully paid;

b) the transfer is not lodged at the company's registered office or such other place as the directors have appointed;

c) the transfer is not accompanied by the certificate for the shares to which it relates, or such other evidence as the directors may reasonably require to show the transferor's right to make the transfer, or evidence of the right of someone other than the transferor to make the transfer on the transferor's behalf;

d) the transfer is in respect of more than one class of share; or

e) the transfer is in favour of more than four transferees.

(6) If the directors refuse to register the transfer of a share, the instrument of transfer must be returned to the transferee with the notice of refusal unless they suspect that the proposed transfer may be fraudulent.

Transfer of uncertificated shares

64. A transfer of an uncertificated share must not be registered if it is in favour of more than four transferees.

Transmission of shares

65. (1) If title to a share passes to a transmittee, the company may only recognise the transmittee as having any title to that share.

(2) Nothing in these articles releases the estate of a deceased member from any liability in respect of a share solely or jointly held by that member.

Transmittees' rights

66. (1) A transmittee who produces such evidence of entitlement to shares as the directors may properly require:

a) may, subject to the articles, choose either to become the holder of those shares or to have them transferred to another person, and

b) subject to the articles, and pending any transfer of the shares to another person, has the same rights as the holder had.

(2) But transmittees do not have the right to attend or vote at a general meeting in respect of shares to which they are entitled, by reason of the holder's death or bankruptcy or otherwise, unless they become the holders of those shares

Exercise of transmittees' rights

67. (1) Transmittees who wish to become the holders of shares to which they have become entitled must notify the company in writing of that wish.

(2) If the share is a certificated share and a transmittee wishes to have it transferred to another person, the transmittee must execute an instrument of transfer in respect of it.

(3) If the share is an uncertificated share and the transmittee wishes to have it transferred to another person, the transmittee must:

a) procure that all appropriate instructions are given to effect the transfer, or

b) procure that the uncertificated share is changed into certificated form and then execute an instrument of transfer in respect of it.

(4) Any transfer made or executed under this article is to be treated as if it were made or executed by the person from whom the transmittee has derived rights in respect of the share, and as if the event which gave rise to the transmission had not occurred.

Transmittees bound by prior notices

68. If a notice is given to a member in respect of shares and a transmittee is entitled to those shares, the transmittee is bound by the notice if it was given to the member before the transmittee's name has been entered in the register of members.

CONSOLIDATION OF SHARES

Procedure for disposing of fractions of shares

69. (1) This article applies where:

a) there has been a consolidation or division of shares, and

b) as a result, members are entitled to fractions of shares.

(2) The directors may:

a) sell the shares representing the fractions to any person including the company for the best price reasonably obtainable;

b) in the case of a certificated share, authorise any person to execute an instrument of transfer of the shares to the purchaser or a person nominated by the purchaser; and

c) distribute the net proceeds of sale in due proportion among the holders of the shares.

(3) Where any holder's entitlement to a portion of the proceeds of sale amounts to less than a minimum figure determined by the directors, that member's portion may be distributed to an organisation which is a charity for the purposes of the law of England and Wales, Scotland or Northern Ireland.

(4) The person to whom the shares are transferred is not obliged to ensure that any purchase money is received by the person entitled to the relevant fractions.

(5) The transferee's title to the shares is not affected by any irregularity in or invalidity of the process leading to their sale.

DISTRIBUTIONS

Procedure for declaring dividends

70. (1) The company may by ordinary resolution declare dividends, and the directors may decide to pay interim dividends.

(2) A dividend must not be declared unless the directors have made a recommendation as to its amount. Such a dividend must not exceed the amount recommended by the directors.

(3) No dividend may be declared or paid unless it is in accordance with members' respective rights.

(4) Unless the members' resolution to declare or directors' decision to pay a dividend, or the terms on which shares are issued, specify otherwise, it must be paid by reference to each member's holding of shares on the date of the resolution or decision to declare or pay it.

(5) If the company's share capital is divided into different classes, no interim dividend may be paid on shares carrying deferred or non-preferred rights if, at the time of payment, any preferential dividend is in arrear.

(6) The directors may pay at intervals any dividend payable at a fixed rate if it appears to them that the profits available for distribution justify the payment.

(7) If the directors act in good faith, they do not incur any liability to the holders of shares conferring preferred rights for any loss they may suffer by the lawful payment of an interim dividend on shares with deferred or non-preferred rights.

Calculation of dividends

71. (1) Except as otherwise provided by the articles or the rights attached to shares, all dividends must be:

a) declared and paid according to the amounts paid up on the shares on which the dividend is paid, and

b) apportioned and paid proportionately to the amounts paid up on the shares during any portion or portions of the period in respect of which the dividend is paid.

(2) If any share is issued on terms providing that it ranks for dividend as from a particular date, that share ranks for dividend accordingly.

(3) For the purposes of calculating dividends, no account is to be taken of any amount which has been paid up on a share in advance of the due date for payment of that amount.

Payment of dividends and other distributions

72. (1) Where a dividend or other sum which is a distribution is payable in respect of a share, it must be paid by one or more of the following means:

a) transfer to a bank or building society account specified by the distribution recipient either in writing or as the directors may otherwise decide;

b) sending a cheque made payable to the distribution recipient by post to the distribution recipient at the distribution recipient's registered address (if the distribution recipient is a holder of the share), or (in any other case) to an address specified by the distribution recipient either in writing or as the directors may otherwise decide;

c) sending a cheque made payable to such person by post to such person at such address as the distribution recipient has specified either in writing or as the directors may otherwise decide; or

d) any other means of payment as the directors agree with the distribution recipient either in writing or by such other means as the directors decide.

(2) In the articles, "the distribution recipient" means, in respect of a share in respect of which a dividend or other sum is payable:

a) the holder of the share; or

b) if the share has two or more joint holders, whichever of them is named first in the register of members; or

c) if the holder is no longer entitled to the share by reason of death or bankruptcy, or otherwise by operation of law, the transmittee.

Deductions from distributions in respect of sums owed to the company

73. (1) If:

a) a share is subject to the company's lien, and

b) the directors are entitled to issue a lien enforcement notice in respect of it, they may, instead of issuing a lien enforcement notice, deduct from any dividend or other sum payable in respect of the share any sum of money which is payable to the company in respect of that share to the extent that they are entitled to require payment under a lien enforcement notice.

(2) Money so deducted must be used to pay any of the sums payable in respect of that share.

(3) The company must notify the distribution recipient in writing of:

a) the fact and amount of any such deduction;

b) any non-payment of a dividend or other sum payable in respect of a share resulting from any such deduction; and

c) how the money deducted has been applied.

No interest on distributions

74. The company may not pay interest on any dividend or other sum payable in respect of a share unless otherwise provided by:

a) the terms on which the share was issued, or

b) the provisions of another agreement between the holder of that share and the company.

Unclaimed distributions

75. (1) All dividends or other sums which are:

a) payable in respect of shares, and

b) unclaimed after having been declared or become payable, may be invested or otherwise made use of by the directors for the benefit of the company until claimed.

(2) The payment of any such dividend or other sum into a separate account does not make the company a trustee in respect of it.

(3) If:

a) twelve years have passed from the date on which a dividend or other sum became due for payment, and

b) the distribution recipient has not claimed it,

the distribution recipient is no longer entitled to that dividend or other sum and it ceases to remain owing by the company.

Non-cash distributions

76. (1) Subject to the terms of issue of the share in question, the company may, by ordinary resolution on the recommendation of the directors, decide to pay all or part of a dividend or other distribution payable in respect of a share by transferring non-cash assets of equivalent value (including, without limitation, shares or other securities in any company).

(2) If the shares in respect of which such a non-cash distribution is paid are uncertificated, any shares in the company which are issued as a non-cash distribution in respect of them must be uncertificated.

(3) For the purposes of paying a non-cash distribution, the directors may make whatever arrangements they think fit, including, where any difficulty arises regarding the distribution:

a) fixing the value of any assets;

b) paying cash to any distribution recipient on the basis of that value in order to adjust the rights of recipients; and

c) vesting any assets in trustees.

Waiver of distributions

77. Distribution recipients may waive their entitlement to a dividend or other distribution payable in respect of a share by giving the company notice in writing to that effect, but if:

a) the share has more than one holder, or

b) more than one person is entitled to the share, whether by reason of the death or bankruptcy of one or more joint holders, or otherwise, the notice is not effective unless it is expressed to be given, and signed, by all the holders or persons otherwise entitled to the share.

CAPITALISATION OF PROFITS

Authority to capitalise and appropriation of capitalised sums

78. (1) Subject to the articles, the directors may, if they are so authorised by an ordinary resolution:

a) decide to capitalise any profits of the company (whether or not they are available for distribution) which are not required for paying a preferential dividend, or any sum standing to the credit of the company's share premium account or capital redemption reserve; and

b) appropriate any sum which they so decide to capitalise (a "capitalised sum") to the persons who would have been entitled to it if it were distributed by way of dividend (the "persons entitled") and in the same proportions.

(2) Capitalised sums must be applied:

a) on behalf of the persons entitled, and

b) in the same proportions as a dividend would have been distributed to them.

(3) Any capitalised sum may be applied in paying up new shares of a nominal amount equal to the capitalised sum which are then allotted credited as fully paid to the persons entitled or as they may direct.

(4) A capitalised sum which was appropriated from profits available for distribution may be applied:

a) in or towards paying up any amounts unpaid on existing shares held by the persons entitled, or

b) in paying up new debentures of the company which are then allotted credited as fully paid to the persons entitled or as they may direct.

(5) Subject to the articles the directors may:

a) apply capitalised sums in accordance with paragraphs (3) and (4) partly in one way and partly in another;

b) make such arrangements as they think fit to deal with shares or debentures becoming distributable in fractions under this article (including the issuing of fractional certificates or the making of cash payments); and

c) authorise any person to enter into an agreement with the company on behalf of all the persons entitled which is binding on them in respect of the allotment of shares and debentures to them under this article.

PART 5: MISCELLANEOUS PROVISIONS COMMUNICATIONS

Means of communication to be used

79. (1) Subject to the articles, anything sent or supplied by or to the company under the articles may be sent or supplied in any way in which the Companies Act 2006 provides for documents or information which are authorised or required by any provision of that Act to be sent or supplied by or to the company.

(2) Subject to the articles, any notice or document to be sent or supplied to a director in connection with the taking of decisions by directors may also be sent or supplied by the means by which that director has asked to be sent or supplied with such notices or documents for the time being.

(3) A director may agree with the company that notices or documents sent to that director in a particular way are to be deemed to have been received within a specified time of their being sent, and for the specified time to be less than 48 hours.

Failure to notify contact details

80. (1) If:

a) the company sends two consecutive documents to a member over a period of at least 12 months, and

b) each of those documents is returned undelivered, or the company receives notification that it has not been delivered, that member ceases to be entitled to receive notices from the company.

(2) A member who has ceased to be entitled to receive notices from the company becomes entitled to receive such notices again by sending the company:

a) a new address to be recorded in the register of members, or

b) if the member has agreed that the company should use a means of communication other than sending things to such an address, the information that the company needs to use that means of communication effectively.

ADMINISTRATIVE ARRANGEMENTS

Company seals

81. (1) Any common seal may only be used by the authority of the directors.

(2) The directors may decide by what means and in what form any common seal or securities seal is to be used.

(3) Unless otherwise decided by the directors, if the company has a common seal and it is affixed to a document, the document must also be signed by at least one authorised person in the presence of a witness who attests the signature.

(4) For the purposes of this article, an authorised person is:

a) any director of the company;

b) the company secretary; or

c) any person authorised by the directors for the purpose of signing documents to which the common seal is applied.

(5) If the company has an official seal for use abroad, it may only be affixed to a document if its use on that document, or documents of a class to which it belongs, has been authorised by a decision of the directors.

(6) If the company has a securities seal, it may only be affixed to securities by the company secretary or a person authorised to apply it to securities by the company secretary.

(7) For the purposes of the articles, references to the securities seal being affixed to any document include the reproduction of the image of that seal on or in a document by any mechanical or electronic means which has been approved by the directors in relation to that document or documents of a class to which it belongs.

Destruction of documents

82. (1) The company is entitled to destroy:

a) all instruments of transfer of shares which have been registered, and all other documents on the basis of which any entries are made in the register of members, from six years after the date of registration;

b) all dividend mandates, variations or cancellations of dividend mandates, and notifications of change of address, from two years after they have been recorded;

(c) all share certificates which have been cancelled from one year after the date of the cancellation;

d) all paid dividend warrants and cheques from one year after the date of actual payment; and

e) all proxy notices from one year after the end of the meeting to which the proxy notice relates.

(2) If the company destroys a document in good faith, in accordance with the articles, and without notice of any claim to which that document may be relevant, it is conclusively presumed in favour of the company that:

a) entries in the register purporting to have been made on the basis of an instrument of transfer or other document so destroyed were duly and properly made;

b) any instrument of transfer so destroyed was a valid and effective instrument duly and properly registered;

c) any share certificate so destroyed was a valid and effective certificate duly and properly cancelled; and

d) any other document so destroyed was a valid and effective document in accordance with its recorded particulars in the books or records of the company.

(3) This article does not impose on the company any liability which it would not otherwise have if it destroys any document before the time at which this article permits it to do so.

(4) In this article, references to the destruction of any document include a reference to its being disposed of in any manner.

No right to inspect accounts and other records

83. Except as provided by law or authorised by the directors or an ordinary resolution of the company, no person is entitled to inspect any of the company's accounting or other records or documents merely by virtue of being a member.

Provision for employees on cessation of business

84. The directors may decide to make provision for the benefit of persons employed or formerly employed by the company or any of its subsidiaries (other than a director or former director or shadow director) in connection with the cessation or transfer to any person of the whole or part of the undertaking of the company or that subsidiary.

DIRECTORS' INDEMNITY AND INSURANCE

Indemnity

85. (1) Subject to paragraph (2), a relevant director of the company or an associated company may be indemnified out of the company's assets against:

a) any liability incurred by that director in connection with any negligence, default, breach of duty or breach of trust in relation to the company or an associated company,

b) any liability incurred by that director in connection with the activities of the company or an associated company in its capacity as a trustee of an occupational pension scheme (as defined in section 235(6) of the Companies Act 2006),

c) any other liability incurred by that director as an officer of the company or an associated company.

(2) This article does not authorise any indemnity which would be prohibited or rendered void by any provision of the Companies Acts or by any other provision of law.

(3) In this article:

a) companies are associated if one is a subsidiary of the other or both are subsidiaries of the same body corporate, and

b) a "relevant director" means any director or former director of the company or an associated company.

Insurance

86. (1) The directors may decide to purchase and maintain insurance, at the expense of the company, for the benefit of any relevant director in respect of any relevant loss.

(2) In this article:

a) a "relevant director" means any director or former director of the company or an associated company,

b) a "relevant loss" means any loss or liability which has been or may be incurred by a relevant director in connection with that director's duties or powers in relation to the company, any associated company or any pension fund or employees' share scheme of the company or associated company, and

c) companies are associated if one is a subsidiary of the other or both are subsidiaries of the same body corporate.

Other specially commissioned briefings from Thorogood

BUSINESS AND COMMERCIAL LAW

Commercial Contracts: Legal principles and drafting

Burnett, Rachel • £145 ISBN: 978-185418702-4

This briefing takes into account relevant legislation and case law. For all points of the law and critical distinctions, you will find crystal-clear explanations and guidelines to a host of case studies illustrating the law and its application.

Commercial Litigation: Damages and other remedies for breach of contract

Ribeiro, Robert • £145 ISBN: 978-185418397-2

A great deal has changed in the last few years... a new emphasis on claims for damages such as loss of business, opportunity, chance, use and data and recent landmark cases have altered the ground-rules. Completely updated, this briefing includes accounts of all the most recent important cases and highlights significant changes in the way that the courts now assess damages.

Corporate Governance

Martin, David • £99 ISBN: 978-185418354-5

This briefing is a clear, accessible and jargon-free analysis of the practical application of Corporate Governance. With short case studies to illustrate legal requirements, the author guides the reader through all aspects of the Corporate Governance programme, concentrating specifically on its use by organisations who are not required to adopt it, such as listed PLCs.

Email: Legal issues 2008

Singleton, Susan • £125 ISBN: 978-185418630-0

One of the biggest changes to office life in the last five years has been the growth of e-mail. On balance a major advantage to businesses, enabling postage charges and time to be saved, but e-mail also comes with certain legal risks.

This report seeks to highlight those areas where employers particularly need to consider relevant risks. However in most cases the risks can be minimised to an acceptable level and nothing with this report should put any employer off letting their employees loose on e-mail. It highlights principal issues which arise and the means to ensure enforcement, in particular, by presenting to employees a coherent e-mail and Internet use policy so they know where they stand.

For full details of any title, and to view sample extracts, please visit:
www.thorogoodpublishing.co.uk

Freedom of Information Act in Practice 2008

Singleton, Susan • £145 ISBN: 978-185418632-4

- Do you want to know how to use the Act to obtain information about your own competitors?
- Are you worried about making your contracts fully confidential?

These and many other issues are expertly dealt with in this valuable new report.

This report shows how businesses can ensure that they don't disclose information inadvertently and how to protect their own information by drafting new contracts in the right way. Susan Singleton has advised many clients in all sectors on the FOIA from a practical standpoint.

International Commercial Agreements

Attree, Rebecca • £99 ISBN: 978-185418286-9

This report appears at an exciting time for international commercial lawyers: new legislation, fresh opportunities – and the challenge of understanding fully how to exploit them.

Recent changes to EC Competition Law have made a significant impact upon parties' freedom to contract commercially, generally giving them greater flexibility. In the field of e-commerce, the EC has issued a welter of laws that are in the course of being implemented into national laws.

The report explains the principles and techniques of successful international negotiation and provides a valuable insight into the commercial points to be considered as a result of the laws relating to:

- pre-contract
- private international law
- resolving disputes (including alternative methods, such as mediation)
- competition law
- drafting common clauses
- and contracting electronically

Software Contract Agreements

Bond, Robert • £145 ISBN: 978-185418692-8

A thorough explanation of the law combined with expert guidance on negotiating and drafting the best contract for your client.

- A clear explanation of the law relating to computer contracts with particular emphasis on software licenses
- A wealth of advice, tips and techniques for successful contract negotiation and drafting
- Leading author: an expert with over 25 years' experience in IP/IT law in a wide range of sectors
- Valuable sample contracts

BUSINESS STRATEGY AND MANAGEMENT

A Practical Guide to Knowledge Management

Brelade, Sue & Harman, Chris • £99 ISBN: 978-185418230-2

An expert but jargon-free guide to enable you to manage the knowledge in your organisation successfully and to identify, gather and use that knowledge to maximum advantage.

Analyse your Business – A performance health check

O'Connor, Carol • £99 ISBN: 978-185418170-1

This briefing offers the tools and techniques for company-wide analysis and is essential reading for business leaders responsible for corporate performance. Its purpose is to put minor issues into perspective and discourage the use of quick fix solutions for bigger problems.

Tendering & Negotiating MoD Contracts

Boyce, Tim • £99 ISBN: 978-185418276-0

This specially commissioned report aims to draw out the main principles, processes and procedures involved in tendering and negotiating MoD contracts. As Tim Boyce writes in the Introduction, 'it is important to realise that the SPI embraces a conceptual shift in the role of the MoD procurers'.

What does this 'huge shift in thinking' mean for contractors? How exactly has the role of MoD purchasing changed? This briefing covers every aspect of competitive tendering, negotiation and contractual negotiations in this new era. There can be few people who combine Tim Boyce's experience and expertise with a gift for explaining issues and procedures with such clarity.

Understanding SMART Procurement in the MOD

Boyce, Tim • £99 ISBN: 978-185418164-0

The main thrust of this report is on issues to do with strategy, organisation and processes. The single most encouraging and exciting feature of the SMART procurement initiative is that it embraces the need to change the culture. There is a commitment within the high political echelon of the MoD to make this change happen. Probably the greatest single challenge is to ensure that this commitment is maintained through the inevitable changes of personality at the political and senior management level.

IT Governance

Norfolk, David • £99 ISBN: 978-185418745-1

This specially commissioned briefing sets out what the latest legislation says and what it means, its impact on the organisation as a whole and on the IT group specifically, and how to implement an effective IT governance initiative in your company.

For full details of any title, and to view sample extracts, please visit:
www.thorogoodpublishing.co.uk

Practical Techniques for Effective Project Investment Appraisal

Tiffin, Ralph • £99 ISBN: 978-185418099-5

How to ensure you have a reliable system in place. Spending money on projects automatically necessitates an effective appraisal system – a way of deciding whether the correct decisions on investment have been made.

Project Risk Management: The commercial dimension

Boyce, Tim • £95 ISBN: 978-185418257-9

This briefing will show you how to fully appreciate all the commercial dimensions of important projects and understand how to identify all the risks during the pre-contract bidding phase.

Strategy Implementation Through Project Management

Grundy, Tony • £99 ISBN: 978-185418250-0

The gap: Far too few managers know how to apply project management techniques to their strategic planning. The result is often strategy that is poorly thought out and executed.

The answer: Strategic project management is a new and powerful process designed to manage complex projects by combining traditional business analysis with project management techniques.

Surviving a Corporate Crisis: 100 things you need to know

Batchelor, Paul • £99 ISBN: 978-185418208-1

Seven out of ten organisations that experience a corporate crisis go out of business within 18 months. This briefing not only covers remedial action after the event but offers expert advice on preparing every department and every key player of the organisation so that, should a crisis occur, damage of every kind is limited as far as possible.

Technical Aspects of Business Leases: Overcoming the practical difficulties

Dowden, Malcolm • £99 ISBN: 978-185418194-7

The purpose of this briefing is to highlight areas where technical issues might lead to practical difficulties, and to give clear guidance to help those involved in property management avoid the pitfalls.

FINANCE

Tax Planning for Businesses and their Owners

Hughes, Peter • £145 ISBN: 978-185418402-3

Written for business owners and managers, this special report offers expert advice on the tax implications of your business decisions – guiding you in making the right business and personal choices for tax reduction.

Trade Secrets of Business Disposals

Pearson, Barrie • £145 ISBN: 978-185418321-7

If you're like most people, you'll only get one chance to sell your business and to capitalise on years of hard work and planning. You can either fluff it, or make sure you get the best possible advisor and become financially secure for life, and possibly very rich. This briefing shows you how to make your business 'investor-ready' for maximum capital return.

Trade Secrets of Business Acquisitions

Pearson, Barrie • £145 ISBN: 978-185418366-8

In this invaluable new briefing one of the City's most successful deal-makers distils 40 years' experience as both principal and advisor. "Losing a deal by adopting the wrong tactics is unforgiveable" he writes, but it happens all too often. This briefing offers both professional advisors and principals the opportunity to transform their rate of success, clarifying hard truths and highlighting avoidable mistakes. It is laced throughout with proven tactical advice to ensure that both deals and post-acquisition management are carried out with maximum success.

VAT Liability and the Implications of Commercial Property Transactions

Buss, Tim • £145 ISBN: 978-185418747-5

The option to tax is a major VAT planning tool but you have got to get the detail right to take full advantage – and getting it wrong can be very costly. This briefing shows you how to plan for maximum advantage and avoid costly mistakes.

EMPLOYMENT LAW

Data Protection Law for Employers 2008

Singleton, Susan • £145 ISBN: 978-185418626-3

This briefing seeks to summarise the application of the Act to the employment discipline. It concentrates on the areas, which are useful and practical to employers by examining the Information Commissioner's Office code of practice. It answers many of the mundane, day-to-day data protections issues that employers and those who are responsible for personal data need to know.

Discrimination Law and Employment Issues

Martin, David • £145 ISBN: 978-185418678-2

The Age Discrimination Act is billed by lawyers as the most significant change in employment law since the 1970s. In addition to sex and race discrimination laws, in the last two years employers have also had to cope with sexual orientation discrimination and religious discrimination. David Martin, an expert on employment law and practice, analyses the practical aspects of dealing with each of the anti-discrimination laws. He demonstrates how to ensure that paperwork and systems comply totally with the law, and he provides a range of helpful case studies to illustrate the key issues and bring them to life.

Effective Recruitment: A practical guide to staying within the law

Leighton, Patricia & Proctor, Giles • £145 ISBN: 978-185418683-6

The ways to undertake the task continue to grow, making the decision as to how best to recruit for a given employment situation more complex. This specialist text is responding to a number of imperatives, including legal ones. There have been, and are, anticipated changes that make it essential that recruitment practitioners act both effectively and within the law.

Employee Sickness and Fitness for Work: Successfully dealing with the legal system

Howard, Gillian • £99 ISBN: 978-185418281-4

Many executives see employment law as an obstacle course or, even worse, an opponent – but it can contribute positively to keeping employees fit and productive. This briefing will show you how to get the best out of your employees, from recruitment to retirement, while protecting yourself and your firm to the full.

Employment Law Aspects of Mergers and Acquisitions: A practical guide

Ryley, Michael • £99 ISBN: 978-185418363-7

This report will help you to understand the key practical and legal issues, achieve consensus and involvement at all levels, understand and implement TUPE regulations and identify the documentation that needs to be drafted or reviewed within the context of a merger, acquisition or disposal.

Navigating Health and Safety Law: Ensuring compliance and minimising risk

Pope, Chris • £99 ISBN: 978-185418353-8

If you have already been challenged by the insurer, inspector, or one of your workforce about the status of your health and safety this briefing will give you a workable answer to questions like Is my health and safety policy legally compliant? How do I avoid being liable for an employees ill health arising from previous employment? Who should carry out safety inspections – is it my responsibility?

Successfully Defending Employment Tribunal Cases

Hunt, Dennis • £99 ISBN: 978-185418267-8

Sweeping changes to the way employment tribunal claims are dealt with have increased the risk of higher costs and more expensive claims. This indispensable report covers all the changes and their implications for HR professionals.

Applying the Employment Act 2002: Crucial developments for employers and employees

Williams, Audrey • £99 ISBN: 978-185418253-1

The Act represents a major shift in the commercial environment, with far-reaching changes for employers and employees. The consequences of getting it wrong, for both employer and employee, will be considerable – financial and otherwise. The Act affects nearly every aspect of the workplace.

Dismissal and Grievance Procedures

Hunt, Dennis • £99 ISBN: 978-185418376-7

This briefing explains what all the regulations say and what steps you need to take to operate effective dismissal, disciplinary and grievance procedures. It covers all the requirements of the Disputes Resolution Procedures that came into effect in October 2004. It tells you where and when the regulations apply – and what you need to do.

Enabling Beyond Empowerment

Williams, Michael • £99 ISBN: 978-185418084-1

By applying the range of practical management techniques detailed in this briefing, you can provide the authority and means to empower in a way that substantially reduces the dangers.

Flexible Working

Williams, Audrey • £99 ISBN: 978-185418306-4

Recent research shows that far too many individuals, as well as firms, are unaware of flexible working rights. How employers and employees deal with them is of crucial – and increasing – importance to both. This briefing clarifies the law, sets out the rights of employer and employee, and offers valuable practical advice on best practice.

How to Turn your HR Strategy into Reality

Grundy, Tony • £99 ISBN: 978-185418183-1

From a diagnosis of HR issues to an analysis of the external and internal future environment of your company and the effect on your human resources – this is practical information aimed at HR and senior line managers.

Internal Communications

Farrant, James • £99 ISBN: 978-185418149-7

There is growing evidence that the organisations that 'get it right' reap dividends in corporate energy and enhanced performance. In these organisations, internal communications have equal status with the external communications functions. This practical briefing will show you how internal communications, taken in their widest sense, can improve the performance of organisations.

Mergers and Acquisitions: Confronting the organisation and people issues

Thomas, Mark • £145 ISBN: 978-185418676-8

Why do so many mergers and acquisitions end in tears and reduced shareholder value? This report will help you to understand the key practical and legal issues, achieve consensus and involvement at all levels, understand and implement TUPE regulations and identify the documentation that needs to be drafted or reviewed.

New Ways of Working

Jupp, Stephen • £99 ISBN: 978-185418169-5

New ways of working examines the nature of the work done in an organisation and seeks to optimise the working practices and the whole context in which the work takes place. It is more about promoting the best ways of doing things than simple cost driven change. Although it emphasises the importance of business and organisation, it spans the concerns of people, property, technology, community and environment.

Power Over Stress at Work

Araoz, Daniel • £99 ISBN: 978-185418176-3

The HR manager can learn how to deal creatively with stress from the information in this briefing and pass on their knowledge down the ranks. He or she will then halt the downward spiral of diffusing stress and produce a more positive knock-on effect – namely to increase the productivity of the entire workforce and reduce absenteeism resulting from this terrible illness.

Reviewing and Changing Contracts of Employment

Phillips, Annelise; Player, Thomas & Rome, Paula • £99 ISBN: 978-185418296-8

The Employment Act 2002 has raised the stakes. Imperfect understanding of the law and poor drafting will now be very costly. This briefing will:

- Ensure that you have a total grip on what should be in a contract and what should not
- Explain step by step how to achieve changes in the contract of employment without causing problems
- Enable you to protect clients' sensitive business information
- Enhance your understanding of potential conflict areas and your ability to manage disputes effectively.

Trade Secrets of Using e-Learning in Training

Bray, Tony • £99 ISBN: 978-185418326-2

Definitely not for 'techies', this briefing is practical and jargon-free – giving you step-by-step skills and processes to enable you to design effective e-learning products with confidence.

Transforming HR

Hunter, Ian and Saunders, Jane • £99 ISBN: 978-185418361-3

The blue-print for the future of HR – how to deliver proven value to your Board, business and colleagues. The briefing is based on interviews with 60 HR leaders from across industry and public and not for profit sectors. The briefing covers HR outsourcing and shared services.

MARKETING, PR AND SALES

Corporate Community Investment

Genasi, Chris • £99 ISBN: 978-185418192-3

Supporting good causes is big business – and good business. Corporate community investment (CCI) is the general term for companies' support of good causes, and is a very fast growing area of PR and marketing.

Defending your Reputation

Taylor, Simon • £99 ISBN: 978-185418251-7

'Buildings can be rebuilt, IT systems replaced, people can be recruited, but a reputation lost can never be regained...The media will publish a story – you may as well ensure it is your story' *Simon Taylor.* 'News is whatever someone, somewhere, does not want published' *William Randolph Hearst* When a major crisis does suddenly break, how ready will you be to defend your reputation?

Implementing an Integrated Marketing Communications Strategy

Hart, Norman • £99 ISBN: 978-185418120-6

Get ahead and stay ahead of your competition through better integration of your marketing communications. Norman Hart was an international consultant, lecturer and author on marketing, advertising and public relations. His books included *The CIM Marketing Dictionary, Strategic Public Relations, The Practice of Advertising* and *Industrial Marketing Communications.*

Insights into Understanding the Financial Media: An insider's view

Scott, Simon • £99 ISBN: 978-185418083-4

This practical report will help you understand the way the financial print and broadcast media works in the UK. It will also provide you with techniques and guidelines on how to communicate with the financial media in the most effective way, to help you achieve accurate and positive coverage of your organisation and its operations.

Lobbying and the Media: Working with politicians and journalists

Burrell, Michael • £99 ISBN: 978-185418240-1

Lobbying is an art form rather than a science, so there is inevitably an element of judgement in what line to take. The best lobbying is always based on accurate, up-to-date information and on a well-argued case, founded on credible evidence, and delivered to the right audiences in the right tone of voice at the right time. Sounds simple, but it isn't. This expert briefing explains the knowledge and techniques required.

Managing Corporate Reputation: The new currency

Dalton, John & Croft, Susan • £99 ISBN: 978-185418272-2

ENRON, WORLDCOM... who next? At a time when trust in corporations has plummeted to new depths, knowing how to manage corporate reputation professionally and effectively has never been more crucial. This briefing shows you how to:

- Develop PR, brands and relationship management as the vanguards of your corporate reputation
- Strengthen your internal as well as external communications
- Improve the effective management of your stakeholders

Practical Techniques for Effective Lobbying

Miller, Charles • £99 ISBN: 978-185418089-6

Understanding the system and the process in which it works is essential to lobbying effectively. Uncoordinated, uncontrolled and badly planned approaches will do more harm than good, and risk antagonising the people you most want to influence. This briefing provides the techniques required for effective lobbying.

Public Affairs Techniques for Business

Wynne-Davies, Peter • £99 ISBN: 978-185418175-6

This briefing shows in practical terms how you can counter potential threats through a professionally structured and implemented public affairs campaign. Today's successful companies recognise that in order to survive and prosper a comprehensive and disciplined approach to public affairs is no longer just a useful asset, it is now a necessity.

Selling Skills for Professionals

Tasso, Kim • £99 ISBN: 978-185418179-4

Many professionals still feel awkward about really selling their professional services. They are not usually trained in selling. This is a much-needed briefing which addresses the unique concerns of professionals who wish to sell their services successfully and to feel comfortable doing so.

Strategic Customer Planning

Melkman, Alan • £95 ISBN: 978-185418388-0

This is very much a 'how to' briefing. After reading those parts that are relevant to your business, you will be able to compile a powerful customer plan that will work within your particular organisation for you. Charts, checklists and diagrams throughout.

Strategic Planning in Public Relations

Knights, Kieran • £145 ISBN: 978-185418225-8

Tips and techniques to aid you in a new approach to campaign planning. Strategic planning is a fresh approach to PR. An approach that is *fact-based* and scientific, clearly presenting the arguments for a campaign proposal backed with *evidence*. This briefing provides valuable tips and techniques to improve your PR and campaign planning.

Successful Competitive Tendering

Woodhams, Jeff • £99 ISBN: 978-185418235-7

To win business, you must make a convincing case. This briefing will help you become more skillful, and more successful in your tendering.

Techniques for Ensuring PR Coverage in the Regional Media: An insider's view

Imeson, Mike • £99 ISBN: 978-185418019-3

This in-depth briefing will give you the tools and techniques you need to enjoy the opportunities offered by the regional and local media. It offers you practical guidance and advice on how to apply them with maximum effect for your next PR campaign.

Order Form

FIVE WAYS TO ORDER

1 Tel: +44 (0)1235 465 500
2 Fax: +44 (0)1235 465 556
3 Email: direct.orders@marston.co.uk
4 Web: www.thorogoodpublishing.co.uk
5 Post: Marston Book Services, 10-12 Rivington Street, London EC2A 3DU

Title	ISBN	Price	Authors	Qty
Commercial Contracts: Legal principles and drafting	978-185418702-4	£145	Burnett, Rachel	
Commercial Litigation: Damages and other remedies for breach of contract	978-185418397-2	£145	Ribeiro, Robert	
Corporate Governance	978-185418354-5	£99	Martin, David	
Email: Legal issues	978-185418256-0	£145	Singleton, Susan	
Freedom of Information Act	978-185418347-7	£145	Singleton, Susan	
International Commercial Agreements	978-185418286-9	£99	Attree, Rebecca	
Insights into Successfully Managing the In-house Legal Function	978-185418174-9	£95	O'Meara, Barry	
Software Contract Agreements	978-185418692-8	£145	Bond, Robert	
Achieving Business Excellence, Quality and Performance Improvement	978-185418018-6	£99	Chapman, Colin & Hopper, Dennis	
The Commercial Exploitation of Intellectual Property Rights by Licensing	978-185418285-4	£99	DesForges, Charles	
Intellectual Property Protection and Enforcement	978-185418054-4	£99	Brazell, Lorna	
Waste Management: The changing legislative climate	978-185418367-5	£69	Hand, Caroline	
Websites and the Law	978-185418331-6	£99	Singleton, Susan	
A Practical Guide to Knowledge Management	978-185418230-2	£99	Brelade, Sue & Harman, Chris	
Analyse your Business – A performance health check	978-185418170-1	£99	O'Connor, Carol	
Tendering & Negotiating MoD Contracts	978-185418276-0	£99	Boyce, Tim	
Understanding SMART Procurement in the MOD	978-185418164-0	£99	Boyce, Tim	

Title	ISBN	Price	Authors	Qty
IT Governance	978-185418745-1	£99	Norfolk, David	
Practical Techniques for Effective Project Investment Appraisal	978-185418099-5	£99	Tiffin, Ralph	
Project Risk Management: The commercial dimension	978-185418257-9	£99	Boyce, Tim	
Strategy Implementation Through Project Management	978-185418250-0	£99	Grundy, Tony	
Surviving a Corporate Crisis: 100 things you need to know	978-185418208-1	£90	Batchelor, Paul	
Technical Aspects of Business Leases: Overcoming the practical difficulties	978-185418194-7	£99	Dowden, Malcolm	
Tax Planning for Businesses and their Owners	978-185418334-7	£145	Hughes, Peter	
Trade Secrets of Business Disposals	978-185418321-7	£145	Pearson, Barrie	
Trade Secrets of Business Acquisitions	978-185418366-8	£145	Pearson, Barrie	
VAT Liability and the Implications of Commercial Property Transactions	978-185418747-5	£145	Buss, Tim	
Data Protection Law for Employers	978-185418283-8	£145	Singleton, Susan	
Discrimination Law and Employment Issues	978-185418339-2	£145	Martin, David	
Effective Recruitment: A practical guide to staying within the law	978-185418683-6	£145	Leighton, Patricia & Proctor, Giles	
Employee Sickness and Fitness for Work: Successfully dealing with the legal system	978-185418281-4	£99	Howard, Gillian	
Employment Law Aspects of Mergers and Acquisitions: A practical guide	978-185418363-7	£99	Ryley, Michael	
Navigating Health and Safety Law: Ensuring compliance and minimising risk	978-185418353-8	£99	Pope, Chris	
Successfully Defending Employment Tribunal Cases	978-185418267-8	£99	Hunt, Dennis	
Applying the Employment Act 2002: Crucial developments for employers and employees	978-185418253-1	£99	Williams, Audrey	
Dismissal and Grievance Procedures	978-185418376-7	£99	Hunt, Dennis	
Enabling Beyond Empowerment	978-185418084-1	£99	Williams, Michael	
Flexible Working	978-185418306-4	£99	Williams, Audrey	
How to Turn your HR Strategy into Reality	978-185418183-1	£99	Grundy, Tony	
Internal Communications	978-185418149-7	£99	Farrant, James	
Mergers and Acquisitions: Confronting the organisation and people issues	978-185418676-8	£145	Thomas, Mark	
New Ways of Working	978-185418169-5	£99	Jupp, Stephen	
Power Over Stress at Work	978-185418176-3	£99	Araoz, Daniel	
Reviewing and Changing Contracts of Employment	978-185418296-8	£99	Phillips, Annelise; Player, Thomas & Rome, Paula	
Trade Secrets of Using e-Learning in Training	978-185418326-2	£99	Bray, Tony	
Transforming HR	978-185418361-3	£99	Hunter, Ian and Saunders, Jane	
Corporate Community Investment	978-185418192-3	£99	Genasi, Chris	
Defending your Reputation	978-185418251-7	£99	Taylor, Simon	
Implementing an Integrated Marketing Communications Strategy	978-185418120-6	£99	Hart, Norman	

Title	ISBN	Price	Authors	Qty
Insights into Understanding the Financial Media: An insider's view	978-185418083-4	£99	Scott, Simon	
Lobbying and the Media: Working with politicians and journalists	978-185418240-1	£99	Burrell, Michael	
Managing Corporate Reputation: The new currency	978-185418272-2	£99	Dalton, John & Croft, Susan	
Practical Techniques for Effective Lobbying	978-185418089-6	£99	Miller, Charles	
Public Affairs Techniques for Business	978-185418175-6	£99	Wynne-Davies, Peter	
Selling Skills for Professionals	978-185418179-4	£99	Tasso, Kim	
Strategic Customer Planning	978-185418388-0	£99	Melkman, Alan	
Strategic Planning in Public Relations	978-185418225-8	£145	Knights, Kieran	
Successful Competitive Tendering	978-185418235-7	£99	Woodhams, Jeff	
Techniques for Ensuring PR Coverage in the Regional Media: An insider's view	978-185418019-3	£99	Imeson, Mike	

YOUR DETAILS

Please note that payment is required before briefings are dispatched. If paying by credit card, the address given below must be that of the cardholder.

Please use BLOCK capitals.

Name ______________________________

Position ______________________________

Company ______________________________

Address ______________________________

____

______________________________ Postcode ______________

Country ______________________________

Tel ______________________________

Fax ______________________________

Email ______________________________

PAYMENT DETAILS

☐ I enclose a cheque for £ ____________ made payable to MARSTON BOOK SERVICES

☐ Please invoice me

☐ Please charge my credit card

☐ Mastercard ☐ Visa ☐ Barclaycard ☐ American Express ☐ Switch ☐ Connect

Card no. ______________________ Expiry date ______________________

Valid from ______________________ Issue number ______________________

Cardholder's signature ______________________________

☐ I have paid by bank transfer [BACS]: Barclays Bank, sort code 20-65-18, account

____

POSTAGE AND PACKAGING

UK: Postage and packaging is FREE • **OVERSEAS**: £10 for the first copy and £5 for each additional copy

Please quote reference: "**Briefing**" when purchasing